ENDORSEMENTS

Amy Howard beautifully captures the dramatic irony of our current lives here on earth in her *Kingdom Ministry Training Manual*. Caught betwixt and between the "already, not yet," we find ourselves groaning for our completeness that is not yet fully revealed yet hinting at the glory yet to come. Caught in the tension we all feel, Amy offers us practical yet deeply spiritual ways to realize the healing that Jesus offers us on this side of eternity. Her manual is wonderfully practical, insightful, and deeply grounded in Scripture and the Christian tradition. A delight to read and, even more so, to realize in our lives!

Dr. David Horn
Director of Ockenga Fellows, Gordon-Conwell Theological Seminary
Author of *Soulmates: Friendship, Fellowship, and Making of Christian Community*
and *Return to the Parish: The Pastor in the Public Square*

I have known Amy Howard for many years, first as an acquaintance and now as a friend. Amy is unusual (I say this fondly) for many reasons: She is not only intelligent and sensitive but a woman who genuinely loves God and people. Her passionate desire to set people free—body, soul and spirit—is one we all can glean from, and Encounter Culture is a labor of love that Amy has perfected over years of experience. Since the early days of John Wimber, I have been involved in healing ministry, and I find this *Kingdom Ministry Training Manual* to be one of the best written on the subject of healing. All who participate in an Encounter weekend will be changed from the inside out. I highly recommend this book and the author.

Rev. Dr. Barbara Lachance
Author of *The Marred Canvas: Identity and Redemptive Creativity*,
The Blank Canvas: Discovering the Masterpiece That You Are,
and *Saying Yes to God*

Amy Howard has captured some fundamental principles to learn how to pray for the brokenhearted. Her love for God and people shines throughout this manual for ministry training. The material is easy to read, understand and apply. The interactive group activations will launch the participants into a lifestyle of doing Kingdom of God works. It is evident Amy is a practitioner of what she teaches—not just a theoretician. The concepts and practices will benefit both the reader and those to whom they minister.

Rev. Dr. Carolyn Allen
Associate Pastor, Heartland Church, Fort Wayne, Indiana
SoulCare Ministries, author of *Journey into Wholeness* and *Life-Changing Questions*

During their time at Imago Dei church in Bangor, Maine, I watched the spiritual impact of the ministry of Amy and Justin Howard through Encounter Weekends. It was one of the biggest joys of my time as bishop of the Anglican Diocese in New England. The course outline and the background material found in this book will be valuable tools for the church for many years to come. This training spills over into the life of the church—not through the creation of some secret, holier-than-thou club, but rather because it creates a transformed community of disciples who can grow in Christ-like vulnerability in the practice of the faith.

The Right Reverend William L. Murdoch,
Founding Bishop,
Anglican Diocese of New England

Kingdom Ministry Training Manual

LIVING IN THE PRESENCE OF THE FUTURE

Amy Howard

Copyright © 2024, 2021 by Amy Howard

All rights reserved. No part of this publication may be reproduced, distributed or transmitted in any form or by any means, including photocopying, recording, or other electronic or mechanical methods, without the prior written permission of the publisher, except in the case of brief quotations embodied in critical reviews and certain other noncommercial uses permitted by copyright law. For permission requests, write to the address below.

www.encounterculturene.com

For more information, write to:
Encounter Culture Mission Collaborative, admin@encounterculturene.com

All Scripture quotations, unless otherwise indicated, are taken from the Holy Bible, New International Version®, NIV®. Copyright ©1973, 1978, 1984, 2011 by Biblica, Inc.™ Used by permission of Zondervan. All rights reserved worldwide. www.zondervan.com The "NIV" and "New International Version" are trademarks registered in the United States Patent and Trademark Office by Biblica, Inc.™

Cover design by Scott Delong
Edited and interior by Rachel L. Hall, Writely Divided Editing & More

Kingdom Ministry Training Manual: Living in the Presence of the Future / Amy Howard. —Updated edition.

ISBN: *979-8-9872953-1-1 Softcover*

Contents

The Encounter Culture	vii
A Note from the Author	ix
A Word to Leaders	xi
Living in the Presence of the Future	1
Scriptural Foundations	7
The Interview	12
Sickness of the Spirit	19
Emotional Sickness	31
Demonic Sickness	40
Physical Sickness	53
Hearing the Voice of God for Ministry	60
Key Scriptures	73
The Good Physician By Charles Fiske	75
Suffering and the Ministry of Healing	81
Ministry Styles	86
Sample Prayers	90
Bibliography & Sources for Further Study	95
About the Author	97

FOREWORD

The Encounter Culture

As a pastor of 35+ years, I have found Encounter Culture to be a true answer to prayer for the Church of our age. I have always believed in the power of God to minister in real and tangible ways, but I have often observed the ways in which we have been conditioned to say prayers over people and then hope for the best. This approach felt lacking and insufficient. However, my experience with encounter culture has been transformative.

The manual you are holding is tastefully and carefully written and filled with doctrinally sound concepts that inspire faith to rise within your soul. As I read through the pages, I found myself spiritually moved to exercise the principles carefully explained by Reverend Howard. I appreciate how simply and practically the book presents a pathway to a genuine encounter with a God who deeply loves us and is more willing to heal us than we may realize. The teachings about God that we have been familiar with truly come to life as we delve into the pages of this treasure. I am immensely thankful for the impact it has had on me.

Throughout my years in ministry, my family and I have faced many trials and pains that lingered for years. Encounter Culture exposed my heart, my pain, and my need for a miracle in my own soul—and I experienced just that. This encounter with God has left me forever changed.

Through Encounter Culture, I have learned the importance of facilitating genuine encounters with God through the Holy Spirit rather than just reciting prayers. The training and community within Encounter culture have had a profound impact on my own life, leading me to commit to implementing these principles within my church community. As a result, I have witnessed the loving presence of God at work in people's lives, guiding them through confession, repentance, deliverance, and healing. The genuine encounters that take place during these sessions are a testament to the power of the Holy Spirit. I am deeply grateful to Amy and Justin Howard for introducing me to Encounter Culture and for their obedience to the God "who is always better than we think He is going to be."

The transformation and impact that Encounter Culture has had on my life are undeniable, and I am dedicated to sharing this experience with others in my church community.

Rev. Matthew B. McIntosh
Pastor of Warwick Hope Assembly of God
Author of the SoulJourn *discipleship system and journal*
Warwick, RI

PREFACE

A Note from the Author

WHEN I WAS IN COLLEGE, I belonged to a kind of community that ruined me for what might be considered normal Western Christianity. A small band of friends and I engaged in nightly intercession and worship, ate together, and fasted and prayed together. Perhaps most unusually, we lived vulnerably with one another, confessing our sins and encouraging one another in the pursuit of Jesus. We were drawn together by our mutual desire to know and experience more of Jesus and to see His Kingdom come on our campus. In between classes and late into the night, we played, studied, prayed, and worshipped. And the Holy Spirit came. God touched us all, and we were transformed.

A marriage, four moves, six vans, six kids, a church plant, a church revitalization, a missions organization, a labradoodle, and twenty years later, I am convinced more than ever that I tasted a little piece of the Kingdom in those early, sweet days of my life in God. During those years, my heart was waking up to the infinite possibilities of life with an infinite Bridegroom-King, and the Father formed the bedrock for my understanding of Kingdom life on this side of eternity.

I confess I've never had much patience with a Christianity that isn't real, raw, and alive. The decades-old pastoral lament, "Real Christianity seems more possible in the church basement on Wednesday night at AA than on Sunday mornings in the pews," moves my heart with compassion, imagination, and maybe just a little motivational anger. And so, *Kingdom Ministry Training Manual* and Encounter Weekends, Kingdom Ministry Training, Aftermath coaching cohorts, and Missionary Pathways: Encounter Culture Mission Collaborative were born.

At Encounter Culture Mission Collaborative, we establish a paradigm for a life filled with radical, safe, authentic vulnerability, transformation, and encounter with the living God. Vulnerability and transformation don't need to be the exclusive experience of a recovery group meeting. Encounter brings the radical change and life-giving community experience of those Wednesday nights but in daylight hours and for everybody. Whether you're taking this course as a three-day seminar or over eight weeks in person or online, we are excited to come alongside you and your team so that you can bring this same powerful, ongoing lifestyle to your family, neighborhood, workplace, or congregation.

If you have enough courage to follow the Holy Spirit out into the wheat field because you hunger for a church body where members are actually being set free from bondage; where "the river rushes to the lowest place" and ongoing freedom translates into mission; where imaginations, bodies, and emotions are continuously being transformed by the Gospel, Encounter Weekends and Kingdom Ministry training is for you.

Join us on a journey of bringing the things that hurt to a God who heals until heaven and earth are one. You will taste and see the possibilities.

Amy Howard
Executive Director
Encounter Culture Mission Collaborative
Eastertide, 2024

INTRODUCTION

A Word to Leaders

Cul·ture: /ˈkəlCHər/: The set of shared attitudes, values, goals, and practices that characterizes an institution or organization.[1]

KINGDOM MINISTRY TRAINING is not primarily about collecting information. It's not about learning how to sprinkle in a little bit of healing prayer at the end of a Sunday morning church service. Kingdom training is about cultural transformation—which means it looks more like getting a little information and then *going*. And not just going to get a few more people to take a class and then telling them to get going in their communities. For leaders, culture change means going first.

To be conduits of transformation, we must ourselves be in a process of transformation. The road to freedom must be lined not by those who look like they have it all together but by those who need the road to freedom and travel it themselves regularly.

---

[1] "Culture." Merriam-Webster online dictionary. https://www.merriam-webster.com/dictionary/culture

The culture of accountability and mutual respect builds on the humility of learning together and discovering the dynamics of the work of the Holy Spirit through his people. This manual should not be used without the following commitments:

1. **A commitment to ongoing transformation**

This involves engaging in vulnerable confession to safe people on an ongoing basis and being a recipient of healing prayer.

2. **A commitment to growth**

None of us has already arrived. In the West, we strongly prefer collecting information over actual risk-taking action. Information and knowledge make us feel safe. By hiding behind studying, rather than actively practicing what we've learned, we can feel like we possess a kind of protection from the sort of overfamiliarity that might make others despise us when they see our weaknesses. When we go first, we risk having people watch us learn on the job. We'd often rather be seen as perfect before we're willing to try.

3. **A commitment to go first in humility, testimony, and stepping out in faith**

Leadership in the Kingdom of God finds its model in Jesus, who chose to be baptized by John at the very start of his public ministry. In his baptism, Jesus identified with those who endured the humiliation of coming clean and even scorned the shame of what others might think. After all, he was sinless and needed no cleansing. When we go first in humility, testimony, and stepping out in faith, we create a safe pathway for others to follow. We establish a culture of humility and emulate Jesus' ministry rather than one that seeks the praise of people.

***

I hope and pray that you will find in this course not simply a collection of techniques and theological ideas but the beginnings of a journey of transformation. In that transformation, you and your community will learn as you go, do the works of Jesus, and grow in intimacy with the Godhead and each other.

Kingdom Ministry Training Manual

KINGDOM LESSON 1

Living in the Presence of the Future

Course Objectives

- Explore the *why* of healing prayer
- Learn about the *how* of healing prayer
- Observe, discuss, practice, debrief, grow

Introduction

THIS BOOK AND ITS ACCOMPANYING SEMINAR provide an introduction to prayer ministry. Participants will:

1. Explore what it means to live as people of the Kingdom of God. We will examine various topics, including why we pray for the healing of hearts, minds, bodies, and spirits;

2. Be introduced to the four categories of sickness and their corresponding models of prayer; and

3. Be equipped by observation, discussion, practice, and debriefing to effectively and lovingly offer ministry to those seeking prayer.

Participants will also be exposed to available resources for further study in healing prayer and prophetic ministry. We will be immersed in the scriptures and have the opportunity to receive and participate in personal, holistic prayer ministry.

Covenant and Kingdom

Covenant and Kingdom are the two themes, like the two strands of DNA, that run through the entire Bible. Not only has God saved us to be someone, but He has also saved us to do something. We've been saved from sin and condemnation and saved for deep communion with God: this is *covenant*. We encounter a God who is our good Father, who imparts to us the identity of sons and daughters. From being rooted and established in that identity, we learn to model ourselves after the nature of Christ in loving obedience.[2]

With this new identity comes a new way of living which is also rooted in the heart of God. This time we encounter God as the great King. Every king has a kingdom, and every kingdom has citizens and a culture. As sons and daughters of the King, we are tasked with representing the King in our spheres of influence to establish the culture of Heaven.

The Kingdom of God: The Way Life Should Be

Jesus taught the following:

1. How to engage the Kingdom: Repent and believe the "Good News"
2. What the Kingdom of God, interchangeably called the "Kingdom of Heaven," looks like
3. Jesus demonstrated and then commissioned his followers to demonstrate the works which establish his Kingdom:
    a. Healing the sick
    b. Driving out demons
    c. Preaching repentance
    d. Teaching obedience to the Father (Matt. 28:18–20)

---

[2] Mike Breen, *Covenant and Kingdom* (Pauley's Island, 3DM, 2010).

Lesson 1: Living in the Presence of the Future

The "Already, Not Yet" of the Kingdom[3]

1. **The Kingdom of God *has come*:** Through the incarnation, earthly ministry, death, resurrection, and ascension of Jesus Christ, the Kingdom of God appeared and was made manifest on the earth.

2. **The Kingdom of God *is coming*:** Through the ministry of the Holy Spirit, the Church continues to advance the rule and reign of God in this age.

3. **The Kingdom of God *will come*:** At the return of Christ when he takes his seat of authority in Jerusalem, the Kingdom of God will ultimately overtake the entire Earth.

Living in the Overlap

Consider the timeline below, based on the work of George Ladd.

Living in the Overlap

The Age to Come

The Church Age	The Millennium	Eternity
The Already, Not Yet		

Creation (*Fall*) — Resurrection of Christ — *Return of Christ; Resurrection of the Dead 1* — Resurrection of the Dead 2

The Old Age

1. We live in the **tension**. This is the time between two diametrically opposed ages.

   a. **Old Age:** From the Fall to the Resurrection of Christ, and, in part, extending through Christ's return. This age is marked by being under the dominion of Satan, and is passing away.

   b. **Age to Come:** Under the complete dominion of Christ.

---

[3] Adapted from George Ladd, *A Theology of the New Testament* (Grand Rapids, MI: Eerdmans, 1974), 48.

2. The **already, not yet**: Until Christ returns, there will always be more to do.

   a. "With all wisdom and understanding, he made known to us the mystery of his will according to his good pleasure, which he purposed in Christ, to be put into effect when the times reach their fulfillment—to bring unity to all things in heaven and on earth under Christ" (Eph. 1:8b–10).

   b. The consummation of natural history, this present age, and the future age is the marriage of Heaven and Earth (Eph. 1:10).

Living in the Presence of the Future

1. The term *Ekklesia* is a Greek word used by New Testament writers to refer to what we now call the Church. The fuller connotation of this word encompasses the ideas of "called out ones, assembly, or church." It points to the reality of a ruling council of a city-state that governs under but along with the King over the King's realm.

2. Being in Jesus makes us covenantally one with Him, meaning we have everything He has. All authority has been given to Jesus by the Father, and so we go in His authority, making disciples of all nations and baptizing them into this new humanity, reign, and reality.

3. Just as when Jesus ministered on earth, the power to declare and demonstrate the Kingdom of God comes from the Holy Spirit, who indwells us. He connects us with the age to come for which we yearn. It is by the Holy Spirit that we "taste the powers of the coming age" (Heb. 6:4–5).

Living in the tension—in the "already-not-yet" of the Kingdom of God, is not easy. We see both the promises of God and the ministry of Jesus alongside our present realities, which include much suffering and even death. Humans are always looking to resolve tension—to make difficulty or confusion go away. Jesus demonstrated what "on earth, as it is in heaven" looked like during his earthly ministry, but our experiences do not always line up with what we see in the ministry of Jesus. To stand in the tension—otherwise known as "faith"—is to practice praying "thy Kingdom come, thy will be done, on earth as it is in heaven," rather than attempting to redefine "on earth as it is in heaven." It can be excruciating to stand in faith and continue to pray for hurting, sick people rather than protect ourselves or others from disappointment if God does not respond immediately or in the way that we envision. But this is truly part of what it means to "carry our cross" (Lk. 9:23)—choosing to live in the place where the conflict between the "already" and the "not yet" is actively taking place, and trusting the outcomes—both the immediate outcomes of our prayers and the ultimate outcomes at the return of Jesus—to the Father.

BREAK-OUT SESSION

- Read Isaiah 61 (see Appendix A: Key Scriptures).
- Further Reading:
    - Mike Breen, *Covenant and Kingdom: The DNA of the Bible*, 111–135.
    - George Ladd, *A Theology of the New Testament* (Grand Rapids, MI: Wm. B. Eerdmans, 1974).

Notes

KINGDOM LESSON 2

Scriptural Foundations

Healing in the Old Testament

1. The people of God in the Old Testament were familiar with the reality that sin often resulted in sickness.

    a. "If you listen carefully to the voice of the Lord your God and do what is right in his eyes, if you pay attention to his commands and keep all his decrees, I will not bring on you any of the diseases I brought on the Egyptians, for I am the Lord, who heals you" (Exod. 15:26).

2. Sickness was seen to be primarily a result of sin.

    a. Consider the accounts of Saul's insanity (1 Sam. 16:14–5) and of Miriam's leprosy (Num. 12:1–10).

    b. Note, though, there are exceptions. No sin is cited, for example, regarding Hezekiah's sickness in 2 Kings 20:1–11 or in the account of Job's illnesses and calamities.

3. Sin, sickness, and judgment are both individual and corporate.

    a. Corporate covenant-breaking results in corporate curses such as illness, defeat in battle, captivity, etc.

b. Corporate covenant-keeping results in blessings such as health, safety, provision, agricultural success, etc.[4]

4. Some examples foreshadow the healing ministry of Jesus and reveal God's relationship with and heart toward Israel under the Old Covenant.

   a. Healing of identity through covenantal relationship: God renames Abraham (Gen. 17), Jacob (Gen. 32), and the people of God through the prophet Hosea (Hos. 2:14–23).

   b. Deliverance: God parts the Red Sea for the Israelites, rescuing them from their oppressors when He closes the waters behind them.

   c. Physical healing, healing from sin: Consider Moses with the snake in the wilderness (Num. 21:6–9) and the healing of Naaman (2 Kin. 5:1–19).

   d. Healing of the mind, heart: See Jeremiah 31:31–34 and Ezekiel 36:24–28.

   e. Healing of the whole person, destiny: See Isaiah 61.

   f. The name *Yahweh Rapha*, first revealed in Exodus 15:26, means "I am the Lord who heals you."

The angel who revealed the divine origins of Mary's pregnancy to Joseph declared that "...what is conceived in her is from the Holy Spirit. She will give birth to a son, and you are to give him the name Jesus, because he will save his people from their sins" (Matt. 1:20b–21). When the second member of the Trinity took on human form, he also condescended to a human name, which revealed something crucial about God's nature and his mission: The name "Jesus" literally means "God saves." The primary word for salvation, *sōtēria*, is used throughout the New Testament for deliverance from sin and its consequences, as well as for healing, such as in Matt. 9:22. New Testament authors frequently merged the language of healing, salvation, and deliverance; "salvation" can now be understood as divine rescue from all manner of sin, pain and alienation associated with the Fall.[5]

---

[4] John Wimber, *Power Healing* (San Francisco: Harper and Row, 1987), 34–43.

[5] Amy Howard, "Biblical Theology: God as a Deliverer in the Old and New Testaments, and the Implications for the Mission of the Church" (Trinity School for Ministry. Ambridge, PA, 12 April 2024).

Healing in the New Testament

1. Jesus always linked healing with a declaration of the Kingdom of God. He said: "But if it is by the Spirit of God that I drive out demons, then the kingdom of God has come upon you" (Matt. 12:28).

2. Jesus and His disciples preached and demonstrated the coming of the Kingdom of God before He died and rose from the dead. This addresses a commonly held belief that Jesus only came to bring eternal salvation after physical death to those who believe in Him. Of course and importantly, this is true, but the "good news" that Jesus preached had a present-day, before-death application that He demonstrated through healing and deliverance. In the latter part of 1 John 3:8, John writes, "The reason the Son of God appeared was to destroy the devil's work." This scripture directs our gaze on the glorious reality of eternal salvation directly through our present experience. Jesus came not only for the future but to destroy every work of darkness, including disease, bondage, and oppression (see also Luke 7:18–23, which describes Jesus' proof to John the Baptist's disciples that He was the awaited one).

    a. Sin and sickness are no longer exclusively linked. Sickness is primarily seen as an extension/effect of sin which demarcates the kingdom of Satan.

    b. Jesus began his public ministry with a proclamation from Isaiah 61.[6] He made it clear that He had arrived to deliver, heal, and restore those held captive in body, mind, and spirit to the kingdom of darkness.

    c. The Kingdom and rule of God are within us (Luke 17:21). The ministry and person of Jesus "brought the age to come into our present evil age."[7] See Galatians 1:4 and Ephesians 1:21.

The Coming Kingdom

1. The coming Kingdom refers to the time when Jesus returns to the Earth to establish His reign and influence throughout every sphere of life. At this time, we will see with our eyes and experience the fullness which began

---

[6] See Luke 4.

[7] Wimber, 34–43.

with the death, resurrection, and ascension of Jesus. It is this reality we pray for when we pray "Thy Kingdom come." We ask for the coming Kingdom to enter our present reality.

2. When His Kingdom comes, all emotional pain, the ravages of sin, physical sickness, and demonic oppression will be gone forever. "He will wipe every tear from their eyes. There will be no more death' or mourning or crying or pain, for the old order of things has passed away" (Revelation 21:4).

3. In the coming Kingdom, men and women will be completely whole.

Divisions of Sickness/Healing

Francis MacNutt, a former Catholic priest and experienced minister of healing, distilled sickness into four categories with four corresponding methods of prayer and, for liturgical communities, the appropriate sacramental response for each. These divisions are not to be seen as a formula but rather as an introduction to the problem and consequences of sin and brokenness. Throughout the following chapters, we will use his categories as a format for study, discussion, and group prayer.[8]

Sickness of the Spirit

- Cause: personal sin
- Corresponding prayer: Prayer of Repentance, Forgiveness, the "4 Rs"

Emotional Sickness

- Cause: emotional hurts and damage from the past
- Corresponding prayer: Prayer for Inner Healing

Physical Sickness[9]

- Cause: disease or accident
- Corresponding prayer: Prayer for Healing

---

[8] Francis MacNutt, *Healing* (Notre Dame, IN: Ave Maria Press, 1974, 2006).

[9] Physical sickness can also be (and often is) linked with the other three forms of sicknesses. Often, inner illnesses will manifest as physical illnesses.

Demonic Oppression

- Cause: "open doors" such as unforgiveness, stinginess, hatred, trauma, occult practice, etc.
- Corresponding prayer: Prayer for Deliverance

FOR FURTHER READING:

- See Appendix B: "The Good Physician," By Bishop Charles Fiske. (From *Back to Christ*.)
- Also, see Francis MacNutt's *Healing*. From Ave Maria Press, 1974.

The Interview

I never give a person both ears anymore.
I just give you one ear, but not my best one.

—Rev. Tommy Tyson, on listening to God
while interacting with others

The corporate body has learned the importance of a diagnostic interview from those who have developed healing ministries in the last sixty years. An interview can be as formal as asking a person to complete a family tree and a spiritual inventory or as simple as asking helpful questions concerning the presenting problem before engaging in prayer ministry. In an interview, the minister listens both to the individual who is hurting and to the Lord. Through listening, a clearer picture develops of what is wrong, what the possible causes are, and what potential solutions might be.

The most important thing in an interview regarding any kind of sin, sickness, or pain is that the one being interviewed and ministered to encounters the opportunity to be loved. **Love is always the central goal of prayer ministry.**

Preparation

As you prepare to interview someone seeking prayer, consider the following suggestions.

- Pray a prayer of protection (see Appendix E: Sample Prayers)
- Establish a neutrally-scented environment (no strong perfumes/colognes; avoid bad breath, body odors)
- Establish an appropriate setting: be aware of your surroundings. If you are praying for healing in line at a grocery store, step out of line, and be aware of those whom you might be obstructing. If you are in a church environment, make an effort to achieve an appropriate amount of confidentiality for the setting. Take into consideration the possible need

for a chair to sit in if the prayer gets long, or the recipient looks tired or unsteady.

- Invite a group of two or more ministers

- Determine one obvious leader

- Know the chain of authority: who can you talk to if something comes up in prayer that makes you feel uncomfortable? In ECMC events, we practice strict confidentiality in regards to what is shared between a prayer minister and the one receiving prayer, with the stated exception that our ministers function as a part of a closed-circuit team and may share with their team or leaders at the event. We want both our ministers and our participants to feel safe and always select a designated leader who needs to be brought into the prayer session if the person receiving prayer reports suicidal ideation with a plan to act or the active abuse of a minor. If you are running a prayer ministry apart from ECMC, it is best practice to know your state laws regarding mandated reporting and have clear reporting and confidentiality guidelines in place for your ministers.

- Acknowledge your goals (*see boxed highlight below*)

Acknowledge your goals: It is helpful to acknowledge that our goals often reach beyond the scope of being loved by God and giving that love away through listening, discernment, and prayer. Being attached to particular outcomes or a timeline for results, rather than choosing to "stand in the tension" by faith, can easily lead to resentment towards God or substituting formulas for prayer rather than humbly listening and following the Holy Spirit. Take a quiet internal moment to notice any goals that you might be carrying into your prayer session, and intentionally release your personal attachment to outcomes and timelines to the Father, who wants healing far more than we do and is committed to loving you and the person you're praying for, perfectly.

Step 1: Establish with the interviewee where or how they hurt

Ask questions such as "How can I pray for you?" and "Where does it hurt?" as well as more specific questions to follow up. This process serves three purposes:

1. Asking questions demonstrates to the person you are praying for that they are worth your attention and the time it takes to minister to them.

2. After you hear the initial answers, you may find it is appropriate to ask them to fill out a survey such as the Encounter Spiritual Profile or a family tree.

3. The answers should help you pray more effectively. A great follow up question often sounds something like this: "What do you want God to do for you?" A question like this can often help bring real clarity.

If you haven't previously known the person for whom you are praying, it is sometimes helpful at this point to explore where they are on their journey with God. What is their current relationship (if any) with Jesus? Have they ever been baptized (in water; in the Holy Spirit)? Sometimes direct, yes/no questions ("So, are you a Christian?") are not as helpful as questions that encourage description and discussion.

During the interview, we listen on both natural and supernatural levels. You can ask helpful internal questions of God: "What are You doing right now? Where are You already at work? How can I best pray for this person? What are Your feelings about this person or their situation? How can I be a conduit of Your love to them?"

Step 2: Prayer selection/diagnostic decision

See *Sicknesses* (particularly the Divisions of Sickness/Healing) and choose corresponding prayers.

Step 3: Pray

Remain open and attentive to what the Holy Spirit is or is not saying. **Always** begin by asking permission to use the following:

- Physical contact. "Do I have your permission to place a hand on your shoulder while I pray?"

- Anointing oil/holy water (if used). "May I anoint you as we pray?"

- Praying/singing in the Spirit. "Is it okay for me to pray in the Spirit?"

Prayer ministers should keep their eyes open while praying. Having your eyes open allows you to maintain awareness of the prayer recipient's reactions to prayer, as well as to maintain your awareness of any manifestations from the Holy Spirit, demonic, or otherwise.

Silence is okay! Plan on being silent and waiting on the Lord. However, remember it is often helpful to ask the recipient for their permission to wait silently. That way, they won't feel confused if they are not used to silent prayer or waiting.

Step 4: Ask for feedback; repeat steps 1–3 if necessary

Questions such as "How do you feel?" and "Is anything coming to mind as we pray?" can help determine the direction of the prayer. If the one receiving prayer responds, "I feel free," or "my knee is totally healed," take time to thank the Lord together. If he or she responds with something such as, "Nothing seems to have changed," or "I still feel heavy," this may be an excellent time to revisit interview questions or wait on the Lord together.

This can also be a great time to bring in another prayer minister if needed. It is important to do this graciously, asking the permission of the person receiving prayer.

> Inviting another prayer minister into the session does not have to be awkward. If you would like to invite someone else to join you, you can say something like: "I know someone who I think would be really helpful to this prayer session; do you mind if I ask them to join us?" Or "I think a fresh set of ears and eyes may be helpful; would you be comfortable with my inviting [prayer minister] to join our prayer?"

It's important to note that we do not tell people that they are free or healed. That determination is left to the individual to determine for themselves. Often, results of healing prayer emerge over time, and we want to respect the experience of the individual, leaving room for God to work at His own pace.

Step 5: Give post-prayer directions, blessing

Keep in. mind that there should be a clear difference between a prayer minister, pastor, or counselor. In a prayer ministry session, we are not giving advice or providing extended pastoral care. But this is a good place during the prayer time to perhaps ask whether the recipient has a good church they are involved in, or recommend a known counselor for continued care.

Step 6: Pray a "cutting free" prayer with your fellow ministers.

Take time to do this once the person you are praying for has left. See Appendix E, Sample Prayers.

***

Things to Keep in Mind

1. People will be more likely to be open, honest, and secure in a **private setting**. A sense of privacy can be established during prayer ministry time in a public worship setting, especially if there is a background of white noise or music worship that lends itself to private conversation. If part of the goal of a worship service is to include personal ministry time, having musicians or sound techs who are sensitive to the needs of the ministry team and those being prayed for is extremely helpful.

2. With any Encounter Culture team, we strongly encourage all prayer ministers to **pray in groups of two or more**. This is for the safety of both the prayer minister and the one receiving prayer. At least one person of the same gender as the person being ministered to should be present. If you happen to be praying alone, and the prayer turns toward deliverance, it is wise to politely request at least one more prayer minister to join. This does not have to be awkward. A statement such as, "With your permission, there is a member of our prayer team with some experience in this area who I would love to invite into this session," usually works well. It is often helpful to pray in two's anyhow, as other intercessors involved may receive words or scriptures from the Lord that the lead pray-er can then use to minister.

3. We stress the importance of having **one obvious leader of a prayer session**, particularly when the session involves deliverance. Those on the prayer team must know who is leading the session. A clear lead gives the one being prayed for a sense of security and a sense of who is in authority. If the team is not in unity (to the best of their ability, with the aid of the Holy Spirit), effective deliverance can easily be undermined by wrestling for control (both by pray-ers and recipients) and confusion. The lead prayer should guide the prayer session and check in visually or verbally with the other ministers for what the Holy Spirit may be saying to them.

4. If you have prayed everything you know to pray and listened for the Holy Spirit on behalf of the one for whom you are praying, and you still feel like you have had little or no success, do not despair! Several things may be taking place, but you may have no knowledge of which (if any) are occurring. The individual for whom you are praying:

    a. May not be being entirely honest about the situation;

    b. May be unaware of underlying causes that need more searching out and/or time to discern;

    c. May not be ready to repent/part with the issue/be healed;

    d. May have so much fear and doubt in a situation that they cannot receive the truths of the Kingdom; and

    e. A variety of other issues may also be at work.

***

Don't be discouraged. John Wimber taught two things that I like to keep in mind: "Faith is spelled R.I.S.K.," and "I would rather pray for 100 people and see 1 get healed or set free, than pray for nobody and see nobody set free."

Notes

KINGDOM LESSON 3

Sickness of the Spirit

Is anyone among you sick? Let them call the elders of the church to pray over them and anoint them with oil in the name of the Lord. And the prayer offered in faith will make the sick person well; the Lord will raise them up. If they have sinned, they will be forgiven. Therefore confess your sins to each other and pray for each other so that you may be healed. The prayer of a righteous person is powerful and effective.

Elijah was a human being, even as we are. He prayed earnestly that it would not rain, and it did not rain on the land for three and a half years. Again he prayed, and the heavens gave rain, and the earth produced its crops.

My brothers and sisters, if one of you should wander from the truth and someone should bring that person back, remember this: Whoever turns a sinner from the error of their way will save them from death and cover over a multitude of sins.

– James 5:14–20

The healing of our spirit, in which our relationship with God is renewed and restored, is the most fundamental area of healing. Without doubt the healing of our spirit is the linchpin around which all other areas of healing revolve.

– John Wimber, Power Healing, *66*

Sin: The Universal Human Condition

1. The Scriptures of the Old and New Testament are clear regarding the painful alienation of sin that has plagued all of humanity since the Fall. In the Old Testament, sin is seen as the source of alienation of humans from God (Isaiah 59:1-4), and as a result, alienation from the earth, other humans, and even life itself (Genesis 3:16-19).

2. Sin and humanity's partnership with sin leads not only to alienation but to shame, fear of death, guilt, and the drive for survival at any cost. The prophet Nehemiah poignantly states that even when Israel is returned to their ancestral land from exile in Babylon, they are still "slaves" due to their personal sin (Neh. 9:36). Jeremiah succinctly diagnoses the pain and alienation at its source: the broken and corrupted human heart (Jer. 19:9–10), and in the New Testament, the Apostle Paul makes sure his readers know that the problem of sin isn't an isolated issue: everybody is at fault, and everybody is broken in a way they cannot fix without Jesus (Rom 3:23).

> A Russian emigre to the United States during the tumultuous years of the 20th Century, Eastern Orthodox philosopher and priest Alexander Schmemann described the Fall of humanity as a series of divorces, or tears that took place between things that once were unified, life-giving, and at peace. He portrayed the pre-Fall world as one in which all created things were designed as a conduit of the presence and knowledge of God, to be enjoyed by humans and offered back up to God with thanksgiving, like a divine electrical circuit. The repercussions of the Fall broke the circuit, rendering all of those original relationships selfish, impotent, and futile rather than brimming with revelation, generosity, and delight.[10]

3. Sins always results in an injured party:

    a. Self
    b. Other individuals
    c. Groups of people
    d. God

Note: Because of the way God links Himself with the suffering of humanity as a result of sin, God is always an (and the ultimate) injured party. God has

---

[10] Alexander Schmemann, *For the Life of the World* (Crestwood, NY: St. Vladimir's Seminary Press, 1997), 14.

inextricably intertwined Himself with both the first and second greatest commandments: love of God and love of our neighbor. Consider the following examples:

- In Paul's encounter with God on the road to Damascus, God asks: "Saul, Saul, why do you persecute *me*?" (Acts 9:4, italics mine).

- In Matthew 25:31–46, God Himself is both the injured and the blessed party because He has so united Himself with the conduct, experiences, and suffering of humanity.

- "But he was pierced for our transgressions, he was crushed for our iniquities; the punishment that brought us peace was upon him, and by his wounds we are healed" (Isa. 53:5).

1. Sin always creates damage. Sometimes the damage is not immediately seen or ever outwardly visible.

2. A lack of proper understanding concerning forgiveness, healing, and reconciliation papers over sin without actually producing healing. More on this later.

3. Sin can cause or be the result of generational sin (i.e., David's sexual misconduct, polygamy, Abraham's lies, etc.)

> *The LORD, the LORD, the compassionate and gracious God, slow to anger, abounding in love and faithfulness, maintaining love to thousands, and forgiving wickedness, rebellion and sin. Yet he does not leave the guilty unpunished; he punishes the children and their children for the sin of the parents to the third and fourth generations.*
>
> *—Exod. 34:6–7*

The prophet Jeremiah described this dynamic as having our "teeth set on edge" because our parents have "eaten sour grapes" (Jer. 31:29). Extensive research is now available demonstrating the ways in which addiction, disease, and even trauma can be passed down from parent to child. Part of the Good News of Jesus, promised Jeremiah, would be that forgiveness, repentance, and healing can stretch back through the generations, disarming the power of generational sin and pain.[11]

4. A downward spiral can result when we do not deal with sins by the power of the Holy Spirit (including those we have committed as well as sins committed against us). When we come to pray for healing, this means that sometimes rather than just the presenting sin or pain, there is a trail of sin, and choices made in that spiral of sin, that need to be brought to Jesus for healing.

5. The repentance ministry of John the Baptist preceded the Earthly ministry of Jesus. It enabled those who had undergone the baptism of repentance to enter into the ministry of Jesus, which was the in-breaking of the Kingdom of Heaven.

> *In those days John the Baptist came, preaching in the wilderness of Judea and saying, "Repent, for the kingdom of heaven has come near." This is he who was spoken of through the prophet Isaiah: "A voice of one calling in the wilderness, 'Prepare the way for the Lord, make straight paths for him.'"*
>
> —John 3:1–3

See also Isaiah 57:15, and the following passage from Colossians:

> *Put to death, therefore, whatever belongs to your earthly nature: sexual immorality, impurity, lust, evil desires and greed, which is idolatry. Because of these, the wrath of God is coming. You used to walk in these ways, in the life you once lived. But now you must rid yourselves of all such things as these: anger, rage, malice, slander, and filthy language from your lips. Do not lie to each other, since you have taken off your old self with its practices and have put on the new self, which is being renewed in knowledge in the image of its Creator.*
>
> —Col. 3:5–10

---

[11] See Zara Raza, Syeda Hussein, et. al, "Exposure to War and Conflict: The Individual and Inherited Epigenetic Effects on Health with a Focus on Post-Traumatic Stress Disorder" vol. 3 (*Frontiers in Epidemiology*, February 16, 2023), as accessed April 2023 at https://www.frontiersin.org/articles/10.3389/fepid.2023.1066158/full; or Rachel Yehuda and Amy Lehrner, "Intergenerational transmission of trauma effects: putative role of epigenetic mechanisms" (World Psychiatry 2018) as accessed April 2024 at https://www.ncbi.nlm.nih.gov/pmc/articles/PMC6127768/.

The Role of a Prayer Minister

The following functions represent the parts prayer ministers and intercessors play in helping others heal from sin sickness.

1. To perform the ministry of intercession.

2. To help discern and identify sin, including sin which may have been renamed, in a compassionate, hope-filled way.

3. To assist in bringing the identified sin to Jesus so the one receiving prayer can receive from Him in return.

Hindrances to Entering Freedom

Sometimes, despite our best efforts to help, those seeking prayer for sin sickness may encounter difficulties finding freedom or release. Below are some common reasons which you may begin to recognize as you pray for others.

1. Being in a grace-haze
   In this state, one might think, "Everything is under grace. I don't need to deal with individual sins."

2. Having a poor understanding of forgiveness

3. Being in an unsafe community
   If this is the case, one might feel shame for repentance.

4. An experience of immature fellowship, in which there is no culture of "walking in the light."

5. Unbelief (particularly when in combination with self-hatred)

6. Being in a state of pride
   In pride, one might have a number of thoughts: "I am too big to fail; I have ruined everything; I need to save face; I am too broken to save," etc.

Roadblocks to Effectively Ministering to Those in Sin

We can encounter issues that limit our effectiveness as ministers and intercessors. Here are a few to watch out for:

1. **Over-familiarity**
   We may think we know more than we do about the person in front of us. We may not see people the way God sees them.

2. **Judgment**

   We may have preconceived judgments about the person or the sin.

3. **Excuses**

   We may be making excuses for our own sin and extending that to others, or we may lack clarity regarding the sin in question. This can be particularly confusing with things such as co-dependency (read: *idolatry*), which often masks as love or holiness.

BREAK OUT SESSION

First read James 5:14–20, provided in Appendix A, Key Scriptures.

Questions to consider

1. In what way does James encourage us to deal with our sins?

2. Does this differ from the ways in which you have been familiar with dealing with sin in your personal life? In your church tradition? Within your family?

3. What role does the intercessor/prayer minister play in this passage?

Notes

The Four R's:
Leading Someone Through Repentance of Sins

1. Repent

Once specific sins have been identified, we must choose to seek the forgiveness of God. When we come to Him by faith, forgiveness is always available. We like to say: "If you can call it sin, you can be set free from it!"

We acknowledge our sin as sin and seek the God who resists the proud but will never deny a broken and contrite heart. (See James 4:6, 1 Pet. 5:5, 1 John 1:9, Deut. 30:11–20.)

Repentance must come from the individual who has sinned. We encourage out loud repentance because speaking aloud brings the sin out of the darkness and into the light where it can be healed. Leane Payne puts it like this:

> *We go into healing prayer as one kind of person, and we come out another. In this action, our will is involved; there are things we do. We kill lusts, we cast off the impure and the unholy, we put on the new. True enough, in His Presence there is grace to do these things, but we do them. You do them. I do them.*
>
> *From time to time I have someone ask me to pray that God will take from them a habitual sin such as adultery, envy, anger, masturbation, or whatever, and I have to say, 'no, I can't pray that way. We will go to prayer right now, and you will look up to God and confess that sin specifically, by name; then you will kill it. You will cast it off like a filthy cloak, and together we will "watch" you do it.' We then deal with this sin through confession and proclamation of forgiveness, and not just with words or from the head. We 'see,' for example, the confessed sin going into Christ crucified. And if there is a block to letting go of this sin, we 'see' it."*[12]

Imagery/the imagination can frequently be a helpful tool if used with wisdom, discernment, and patience. One can imagine a picture of sin, and one can imagine letting go of that sin. The imagination, like all things in the created order, was made for encounter and intimacy with God. Part of healing prayer is using our imagination to listen to God and also to welcome Him into our pain by asking Him to show us where He was when harmful things were taking place, what He was doing, etc. If people are unable to "see" Him, this can indicate a wound in the relationship which can then be addressed by prayer.

---

[12] *The Healing Presence* (Grand Rapids, MI: Hamewith Books, 1995), 109.

Repentance must be coupled with belief, even if that belief is only present in the smallest gesture.

After John was put in prison, Jesus went into Galilee, proclaiming the good news of God. "The time has come," he said. "The kingdom of God is near. Repent and believe the good news!" (Mark 1:14–15)

If you or the one for whom you are praying feels "stuck" or cannot reconcile with the idea of having sin that needs forgiveness, directing your/their attention to the sins of the older brother in Luke 15 may be a helpful starting point. (It reveals issues such as legalism/self-righteousness, pride, judgments, fear, self-pity, bitterness and unforgiveness.) Psalm 139:23 might be another good place to begin: "Search me, O God, and know my heart! Test me and know my thoughts."[13]

Areas of sin regarding sexuality are frequently difficult to confess because they are often covered in deep shame. They strike at some of the deepest, most vulnerable places of our being.

2. Renounce

Do you renounce the devil and the spiritual forces of wickedness that rebel against God?

Do you renounce the empty promises and deadly deceits of this world that corrupt and destroy the creatures of God?

Do you renounce the sinful desires of the flesh that draw you from the love of God?[14]

a. Renunciation is the act of saying, in effect, "I don't want it to be this way anymore. I'm laying this down. I'm breaking agreement with the enemy in this place of acknowledged sin."

b. The will is involved. Watch out for passive language (i.e., "Please take this sin away from me."). Favor active, first-person language which takes responsibility ("I willingly…")

c. Identify places of bondage, fear, anger, residual pain, etc., where the enemy can and surely will traffic, and encourage active statements (i.e., "I

---

[13] Neal Lozano, *Unbound* (Grand Rapids, MI: Baker Publishing Group, 2003), 63.

[14] The three renunciation statements listed remain a central part of the liturgies of the Catholic, Orthodox, and Anglican baptismal rites.

repent of sleeping with my girlfriend; I renounce fornication; the fear of loneliness," etc.)

   d. Be aware that the enemy works on a purely legal system with our hearts and lives.

3. Release

   a. We do not just set sin aside; we give it to Jesus at the cross and leave it there with Him.

   b. There are two potential aspects of releasing sin:

      i. We send our own sins to the cross;

      ii. We release people, self, others, God, to Jesus as we forgive them.[15] *[See the footnote below for more on forgiveness.]*

   c. Remember, forgiveness is a choice; healing is a miracle. Forgiveness is the part that we play when we have sinned, or have been sinned against. Healing is God's prerogative. This can go a long way towards explaining why sometimes things continue to hurt, even after we have sincerely repented and/or forgiven. Sometimes thinking about this dynamic in the physical realm rather than the verbal, emotional, or judicial realm, is helpful. If someone came up to you and broke your leg, you can immediately forgive that person and release their sin to Jesus. But unless God intervenes with expedited healing, your leg may still continue to hurt for some time. And the time that it takes to heal does not mean that God isn't listening: it was His idea to create bodies that want to heal, and His power that allows them to do so. Remember, most things in the Kingdom of God are compared to seeds that grow slowly (Mt 13:31–32; Mk 4:26–29), rather than instantly.

   d. Forgiveness is not to excuse bad things that have happened or the people who did them. Forgiveness is releasing those people/things to Jesus and entrusting them to His justice rather than reserving the right to our own justice.

---

[15] We release God to Jesus, not that God has sinned, but we release God from our judgment. Often the most painful part of damaging circumstance is the thought that God could have prevented our pain, but did not, and we get stuck in a place of unforgiveness toward God. We must be reconciled to God in the places where our heart accuses Him of not showing up the way we needed/wanted him to.

4. Receive

    a. In this great exchange, we receive something new from Jesus in place of our sin and pain.

    b. Receiving is crucial. The point of repentance is not simply to get rid of bad things. It is to be united with Christ and receive Him and His life rather than our brokenness. Repentance without reception is at its best incomplete and, at its worst, dangerous. The gate ("repentance unto salvation") is nice, but it needs to lead us somewhere (open pastures, a new identity, and a growing relationship with the Trinity).

    c. Imagery is often helpful. If we can picture the reality of things in our minds, they become real to us in a way that they would otherwise not. We are called to love God with our whole heart, soul, mind, and strength. Imagining truth is a part of this.

    d. If self-hatred or unforgiveness still lurks, this is where you will often find it. It is difficult to receive something excellent with a spirit of self-hatred.

KEY QUESTIONS

1. What do you want Christ to do for you?

2. What does Jesus want you to do?

FOR FURTHER READING

Francis MacNutt's *Healing* (1974) and Mario Bergner's *Setting Love in Order* (1995).

- What is the "cross carrying" that is described (and takes place) in these two excerpts?

Notes

KINGDOM LESSON 4

Emotional Sickness

Inner healing is simply cooperating with the Lord to let Him cure and remove from our psychological natures the things that are blocking the flow of the Holy Spirit.

—Dennis Bennet[16]

FOR INNER HEALING to take place, emotional and psychological pain need to be addressed. This type of pain resides in memories, feelings, and even the body. This pain forms barriers to growth in wholeness, love, freedom, and maturity in Christ. The scriptures call these barriers strongholds. A stronghold is any defense structure we build around an area of wounding or deficiency to prevent being hurt again or to keep from losing the little we feel that we have.

Paul addresses strongholds:

> *For though we live in the world, we do not wage war as the world does. The weapons we fight with are not the weapons of the world. On the contrary, they have divine power to demolish strongholds. We demolish arguments and every pretension that sets itself up against the knowledge of God, and we take captive every thought to make it obedient to Christ.*
>
> *–2 Cor. 10:3–5*

---

[16] Quoted in John Wimber's *Power Healing* (San Francisco: Harper and Row, 1987).

Strongholds can take the form of the emotional "scaffolding" we create as children to help us deal with trauma, abuse, or deprivation. These scaffolds can look like needing to act as the responsible adult in every situation (to maintain control), keeping the peace at all costs (to prevent unsafe relationships or reactions in people), overactive defense mechanisms (to prevent injury), etc. Often, strongholds lead to lifestyles of sin, emotional and relational trouble, and even physical illness. If left unaddressed by the healing love of Jesus, emotional pain and the strongholds surrounding it can be passed down through the generations.

> Strongholds are essentially our mind and heart's way of saying "I've been hurt here before, and I am going to do everything in my power to protect myself from being hurt again," or, "I am terrified of being hurt even if I have never experienced pain here, and so I will create these defensive systems (strongholds) to protect myself from pain, loss, or humiliation."

Sources of Emotional and Psychological Wounding

There are three categories of damaging experiences which may lead to emotional or psychological wounding.

1. **Damage from living in the broken world:**
   Broken world experiences are the result of living in the world. Inherited diseases, poverty, and accidents are just a few examples. Such experiences are entirely beyond our control.

2. **Wounds inflicted by other people:**
   These wounds may be intentionally or unintentionally inflicted.

   a. Some of the most profound are those inflicted (intentionally or unintentionally) by parents and other leadership figures, especially those during infancy, childhood, and teenage years.

   b. They can involve incidents of mental, physical, and emotional abuse, rape, and incest.

   c. Some incidents, such as things said or done by siblings, peers or teachers in grade school, etc., may at times be dismissed as silly, but they can carry significant weight and pain. Or, they may begin protracted trajectories of pain.

3. **Damage from sins we ourselves commit:**
   Even after sin is repented of, frequent guilt feelings need healing. This type of sin might include:

   a. Behavioral sins such as fornication, adultery, homosexual acts, abortions, lying, stealing, etc.;

   b. Sinful attitudes, such as greed, jealousy, selfishness, codependent behaviors (protecting others from the consequences of their sin, creating false or sinful relational systems)[17];

   c. These can also be rooted in false identities or come from pride resulting in resentment and bitterness when our overinflated expectations of ourselves are unfulfilled.

Broken Lenses

Emotional sickness distorts how we perceive what is true about the following:

- Ourselves;
- Others;
- God.

It also creates the seedbed for (among other things):

- Transference;
- Image Distortion;
- Idolatry.

The Goal of Inner Healing: Orthopathy

Orthopathy: *the state of having rightly ordered, operating, and integrated emotions.*

You can think of orthopathy literally as "right feeling." However, applying *right* and *wrong* language concerning feelings is tricky. We should avoid shaming others and move toward providing people an environment where they feel safe enough

---

[17] False or sinful relational systems may take the form of triangulated, codependent, or otherwise idolatrous relationships. These are systems which create the illusion of love, while actually harboring idolatry or delusion.

to process their feelings in order to get to a state of orthopathy. Following up with check-in questions regarding what the person heard you say regarding feelings can help ensure understanding.

The healing journey towards orthopathy addresses:

1. **What we feel:**
   In order to experience the full range of human emotions without fear, shame, or condemnation necessitates removing any blocks that prevent us from experiencing certain (or any) emotions. Those who live not as orphans but as sons and daughters are secure in love and are able to experience and accept emotions for what they are.

2. **How we experience feelings:**
   The head and the heart must be reconnected. We need to renew our ability to not simply rely on information about God, ourselves, and others; we need to experience that information at a heart level.

3. **How we feel about our feelings:**
   We need to have emotional reactions which instinctively work correctly. This does not mean simply counting to ten whenever we're angry in the hopes of not responding to a situation in anger, although it may be a good first step. Anger, per this example, is an emotion that is neither right nor wrong. Healed, right-functioning anger is just one emotion that helps us live a full and free life in Christ. Healed emotions help point us to truth, live separate from but healthfully connected to other people, encounter God, and work together with right actions. Consider these examples:

    a. If my emotions are unhealed, perhaps when I am sinned against, I immediately feel shame instead of anger. Perhaps anger is present, but the anger itself makes me feel "bad." Instead of anger serving its good purpose of separating me from things that would hurt me and working to bring about justice, my guilt thrusts me toward bad situations, and I receive the sins of others into myself willingly.

    b. Grief, sadness, and tears are part of what it means to be human and to love in a broken world. But when an occasion that produces grief arises, if I judge my tears or sadness as weakness, I suppress grief and thus work to reject my own feelings, often through anger.

4. **How we respond to our feelings:**
    We need the ability to respond in the grace of God and the power of the Holy Spirit to the information we receive through emotions. Both the information and our responses are subject to the truth of God rather than our experiences (Rom. 8:1–2; 12:3). Inner healing should help to re-educate us as to who we are in Christ. Who we are, who God is, and how we experience these realities come into alignment with the Word of God and the saving work of Christ.

INNER HEALING FREES US to be able to choose to believe what is true by:

- Disarming the power of negative experiences and memories;

- Removing the sting and shame;

- Bringing justice to pain.

The Kingdom definition of justice is the putting of things to right when God is made King. Justice takes place when God heals hurts in such a way that things are better than they would have been if the hurts had never happened.

Memories Addressed Through Inner Healing Prayer

Two kinds of memories can be addressed in inner healing prayer. These are surface memories and root memories. See the chart below.

Surface Memories	*Root Memories*
Present to the conscious mind	Not necessarily present to the conscious mind; can begin as early as conception
Usually connected to the emotions they contain	Can be emotionally dissociated
Can be experienced and/or contained in the mind, body, and emotions	Can be contained in the mind, body, and emotions; the person is not necessarily aware of how/where
"The *thing* is actually the *thing*"	Often the source or seedbed for other, progressive woundings; "the *thing* is not actually the *thing*"

God's Role and Ours in Inner Healing

1. God:
   a. Sheds light on the source of pain
   b. Gives understanding about the pain
   c. Receives the pain into the body of Jesus
   d. Heals the pain/sting/shame
   e. Repackages the memories through the lens of His love

2. We:
   a. Cooperate with the grace of God
   b. Follow the pain trail
   c. Ask for revelation from the Holy Spirit
   d. Forgive
   e. Repent
   f. Have patience
   g. Practice faith

Praying for the Healing of Emotional Pain

Making use of the imagination is often very helpful in the healing of memories and emotional pain. This often takes the form of encouraging the one being prayed for to "see" (imagine) themselves with Jesus during the painful memory. We can ask questions such as "Where do you see Jesus in the room? What is He doing? Is there an expression on His face?"

> *The Spirit of the sovereign LORD is on me, because the LORD has anointed me to... bind up the brokenhearted.*
>
> *– Is. 61:1b*

1. If the person for whom you are praying is stuck in pain, they often will not be able to imagine Jesus in any helpful way. They may say, "I see Jesus, but He is in the other room, ignoring me," or "No, I cannot see or sense Jesus at all."

2. If this occurs, ask lots of questions to see if the source of the pain surfaces. For example, you can ask, "How do you feel?" "Would you like to forgive yourself (the person who hurt you…Jesus)?". Make sure to listen to the Holy Spirit's promptings.

3. It is appropriate to ask Jesus to enter that memory with the person receiving prayer.

If the person receiving prayer can "see" Jesus, it is often helpful to have them imagine the following:

- Handing hurtful people/sin/pain/shame/false names to Jesus.

- Picturing Jesus on the cross, where sin and pain can be placed directly into his wounds, is often very helpful.

Remind them the pain must go somewhere, and Jesus is the only safe place for it.

Don't forget the fourth "R"—Receive. Often, waiting in that place of imagination, and receiving new things from Jesus in exchange for the old, is very healing.

Healing Emotional–Body Connections

Often, unhealed emotional pain locates itself in areas of the body. Suppose the communication between those different areas of the body is poor or non-existent. In that case, it is important to pray for healed connections between the different parts of the body and the healing of the memories themselves. Consider especially the following:

1. Head
2. Heart
3. Gut
4. Reproductive system

When productive anger is absent or underdeveloped, individuals are often prone to retaining rather than expelling pain as an incident or lifestyle.

You might wonder: does it matter whether the memories are real? Not particularly. However, it is important on the part of the prayer minister not to project or suggest incidents that have not been brought forward by the prayer recipient. It does not necessarily matter whether the memories or impressions the prayer recipient brings up are entirely accurate. No matter the legitimacy of the memory, the end goal is to bring any and all pain and trauma to Jesus.

> *Praise be to the God and Father of our Lord Jesus Christ, who has blessed us in the heavenly realms with every spiritual blessing in Christ. For he chose us in him before the creation of the world to be holy and blameless in his sight.*
>
> *– Eph. 1:3–4*

FOR FURTHER READING:

See: Appendix D, Ministry Styles

- Bessel van der Kolk, *The Body Keeps the Score: Brain, Mind and Body in the Healing of Trauma* (New York, NY: Penguin Random House, 2015).

- Aundi Kolber, *Try Softer: A Fresh Approach to Move Us out of Anxiety, Stress, and Survival Mode--and into a Life of Connection and Joy* (Carol Stream: IL, Tyndale Refresh, 2020).

Notes

KINGDOM LESSON 5

Demonic Sickness

*Blessed be the Lord, the God of Israel;
he has come to his people and set them free.*[18]

Healing from demonic sickness = Deliverance Ministry.

The point of deliverance ministry is always love.

MUCH INFORMATION IS AVAILABLE in Christian and non-Christian literature, media, and educational materials regarding deliverance from the influence of evil spirits. Unfortunately, many of these materials—even in the Christian realm—focus on the sensational, the graphic, and the demonic itself.

The focus of deliverance ministry is, and always should be, love—the Kingdom of God breaking in on the kingdom of darkness to set sons and daughters free to live out their identity in Christ. The measure by which we evaluate the success of deliverance ministry is, in part, the resulting freedom from bondage to and undue

---

[18] From "The Song of Zechariah." From Antiphon, © 2001, GIA Publications and The International Commission on English in the Liturgy. Note: The quoted portion here is based on Luke 1:68.

influence of evil spirits. But success in deliverance ministry is also giving the ones to whom we minister the opportunity to feel safe and loved.

What Is Being Addressed in Deliverance Ministry?

1. Freedom from demonic influence, entities, weapons, and/or wounds that afflict any or all aspects of our humanity (mind, heart, body, relationships, etc.). Demonic affliction occurs along a spectrum of influence; the greater bondage, the less volition an individual experiences in the personal choices, attitudes, and perceptions. The more influence the demonic has, the harder it is to say "no" to that influence.

2. The closing of "open doors" to the demonic. These can be areas of pain, lies, deficiency, trauma, sin, or occult activity through which the enemy can traffic.

3. Restoring potential for intimacy with the Father, Son, and Holy Spirit. Demonic affliction often limits or prevents growth in loving communion with the Trinity.

Essential Realities for Deliverance Ministry

1. The enemy (Satan and his minions) works within a purely legal system. To maintain access to unhealed places in our hearts, minds, and bodies, the enemy uses traumatic events, the seduction of sin and pain to tell us lies about ourselves and God.

2. The enemy works in the dark. Verbal confession/renunciation of sin to another person is often necessary before God can bring light to a situation. It's important to note: If you can call it sin, you can get set free from it.

3. Sin and the pain from sin is a set sum.

4. Sin and pain attract more sin and pain.

5. The only safe place for sin and the resulting pain is the body of Jesus Christ.

6. Jesus paid the price for all sin, trauma, and associated pain in his body on the Cross.

7. In Christ, our will—our ability to choose life over death and holiness over sin—is restored to us.

Sources of Demonic Influence and Bondage ("Open Doors")

Four primary sources open the door to demonic influence:

1. Trauma;

2. Curses and vows (generational or otherwise);

3. Sin/unforgiveness;

4. Occult practices.

When we suspect demonic influence, we need to try to identify the open door(s).

> Alan Kreider, in his recent book *The Patient Ferment of the Early Church: The Improbable Rise of Christianity in the Roman Empire*, describes the religious milieu of Ancient Rome in terms remarkably familiar to those of the 21st-century Western world: "In the competitive religious market of the ancient Roman Empire, a new religion could succeed only if it 'worked.' People would join it only if it contributed something to their experience that made a difference in their lives, that rescued them from things that trapped them, and that brought them to greater wholeness….this is where exorcisms fit in." Kreider goes on to describe the regularly practiced exorcisms of the early church as primarily individual, aimed at "restor[ing] wholeness to people who had been torn apart." Exorcism was seen as an essential part of coming to faith: being cleansed from the demonic and toxic elements of a broken world so the space that had formerly been taken up by the forces of evil could be filled with the whole and free self, and that self then filled with Christ.[19]

1. **No Salvation**
   If a person is not saved, they are under the dominion of darkness (see Eph. 2:1–6; Heb. 2:14–15).

2. **Believing Lies**
   The enemy is the accuser, so the lie or lies often take the form of an accusation. That accusation may be:

   a. About how God acts toward us;
   "God is not good; God doesn't care; God isn't there for you," etc.

---

[19] Alan Kreider, *The Patient Ferment of the Early Church: The Improbable Rise of Christianity in the Roman Empire* (Grand Rapids, MI: Baker Academic, 2016), 113–14; 181–2.

b. About ourselves;
"I am worthless, ugly, unforgivable; I am my disease," etc.

c. About our relationship to God;
"God could never love a person like me. I am the only person at fault here, so I must pay the price [instead of releasing this to the Cross]. I am too messed up, too broken, too mentally ill to save," etc.

d. From others toward us.
We can feel accused through others' unforgiveness, suspicions, judgments, their direct accusations toward us.

3. **Traumatic Memories**
Anywhere pain from past trauma lingers can be a source of demonic traffic.

4. **Willful Disobedience; Occult Activity, Sexual Sin**

5. **Unforgiveness**
Often the lie in not forgiving others is that we create a sense of self-protection and justice through it. We can believe that not forgiving will keep us safe from further injury.

6. **Physical Pain**
The enemy can traffic in physical pain, deformity, and sickness by accusing God of inflicting that pain, and encouraging us to believe alternate realities about our well-being, the good design of God, and the heart of God toward creation. We might believe things such as "God wants me to be broken," or "I am an accident God is just trying to make something good out of." Under the enemy's influence, we may take on our pain and sickness as our rightful identity: "I am my sickness," "God has given me the gift of dyslexia," etc.

7. **Darts and Other Demonic Weapons**

Finally, be strong in the Lord and in his mighty power. Put on the full armor of God, so that you can take your stand against the devil's schemes. For our struggle is not against flesh and blood, but against the rulers, against the authorities, against the powers of this dark world and against the spiritual forces of evil in the heavenly realms. Therefore put on the full armor of God, so that when the day of evil comes, you may be able to stand your ground, and after you have done everything, to stand. Stand firm then, with the belt of truth buckled around your waist, with the breastplate of righteousness in place, and with your feet fitted with the readiness that comes from the gospel of peace. In addition to all this, take up the shield of faith, with which you can extinguish all the flaming arrows of the evil one. Take the helmet of salvation and the sword of the Spirit, which is the word of God.

—Eph. 6:10–17

Open Doors Perpetuate Pain

1. There is only one safe place for pain: Jesus

2. Demonic presence in someone's life:

    a. Inhibits the need/ability to "digest" experiences, good or bad (i.e., the body's natural responses such as shaking, tears, vomiting, righteous anger, etc.);

    b. Encourages the damaged processing of pain, such as:

        i. Transferring pain to others through practices such as raging, abusing, and acting manipulatively;

        ii. Ingesting the pain of others through codependent behaviors ("If I don't keep the peace, rather than draw boundaries with poor behavior, everything will fall apart.");

    c. Attracts more pain.

Examples of Demonically Preserved Pain

1. **Incomplete, chronic grief**
   The grieving process allows pain to be digested by our bodies, minds, and emotions. Tears (when productive) carry the toxins and pain of loss out of our system and can attract loving care from those around us. Godly sorrow unites us to Jesus, and it becomes a source of connection and friendship with a God who suffers.

2. **Co-dependent pain consumption**
   When keeping someone else's pain feels like love, the relationship has likely become co-dependent.

3. **Pain as identity**
   "I am my illness."

4. **Pain lodged in unforgiveness, soul ties**

5. **Pain as justice**
   "I deserve this; it was my fault." "God primarily wants me to suffer for my sins, not to heal my pain."

Open Doors in the Mind

1. The enemy accuses:

    a. Us to ourselves: "You are bad."

    b. Us to God: "God thinks you're bad."

    c. Others to us: "Other people are bad."

    d. God to us: "God is bad."

2. These lies are often rooted in negative experiences.

3. Lies also serve to distort our understanding: "God made me this way." "My disorder is a gift." "My mental illness is just my cross to bear."

Open Doors in the Heart

1. Generational patterns of idolatry, emotional bondage

2. Traumatic memories

3. Soul ties

4. Broken/wounded/non-existent pathways for emotions in the body

5. A misplaced sense of well-being
   Ask, where is my "ok"? Is it in me as I am in God, or am I not "ok" unless other people around me are "ok"?

Open Doors in the Body

1. Curses, witchcraft (intentional or unintentional)

2. Sin involving the body

3. Addictive/disordered pathways in the brain

4. Traumatic incidents often attract pain (until the trauma is healed)

5. Mysterious pain or wounds which will not heal

6. Unexpelled pain can become a source of demonic affliction

Hallmarks of Demonic Affliction

Please note: discernment is needed in these areas. The following list is neither exhaustive nor meant to be diagnostic. This means that just because you witness one or more of these symptoms does not necessarily mean that there is a demonic element to someone's pain. It is critical to remain attentive to the Holy Spirit and the individual for whom you are praying rather than jump to conclusions.

1. Irrationality (You can't reason unto freedom)[20]

2. Mysterious, chronic, sometimes moving pain

3. Stubborn unbelief, hopelessness, accusation, cyclical thinking

4. Addictive behaviors

5. Poorly defined or lack of personal boundaries

6. Habitual or compulsive self-destructive behaviors (compulsively failing, workaholism, self-mutilation, self-injurious behavior, compulsive relationship destruction)

7. Habitual or compulsive destructive behavior towards others (rape, incest, murder, verbal/emotional/physical abuse, violence, rage, compulsive lying, seductive manipulation)

8. Unexplained blackouts

9. Dead or extremely dissociated emotions

---

[20] When someone is demonically afflicted, often the evidence that there is "outside intelligence" is that the person becomes irrational about their pain/victimization/situation. Their arguments will shift consistently as the demonic seeks to retain its influence. There are no solutions, no matter what you offer or counsel—because the problem isn't just irrational, it's demonic.

Praying for Deliverance

When we assist others in deliverance, we are helping them to take responsibility for their lives and respond in faith to Jesus.

—Neal Lozano, Unbound: A Practical Guide to Deliverance[21]

For I am convinced that neither death nor life, neither angels nor demons, neither the present nor the future, nor any powers, neither height nor depth, nor anything else in all creation, will be able to separate us from the love of God that is in Christ Jesus our Lord.

—Rom. 8:38–9

Deliverance is ongoing in the life of a disciple of Jesus. Much of it is accomplished by the grace of God as we apply it to our hearts, minds, bodies, and lives through various helpful practices such as scripture study, prayer, confession of sin, worship, and receiving the sacraments.

The renunciation of the devil and breaking off the power of evil spirits through renunciation and command are addressed below. This often takes place best in a 2 to 3-person team with a clear leader, while others serve as intercessors and support.

Before beginning, it is essential to know who He is and what He has done:

He forgave all our sins, having canceled the written code, with its regulations, that was against us and that stood opposed to us; he took it away, nailing it to the cross. And having disarmed the powers and authorities, he made a public spectacle of them, triumphing over them by the cross.

—Col. 2:14–5

Additionally, you need to know who you are and what you are called to do.

The Spirit of the Sovereign Lord is on me, because the LORD has anointed me to proclaim good news to the poor. He has sent me to bind up the brokenhearted, to proclaim freedom for the captives and release from darkness for the prisoners, to proclaim the year of the Lord's favor and the day of vengeance of our God, to comfort all who mourn, and provide for those who grieve in Zion—to bestow on them a crown of beauty instead of ashes, the oil of joy instead of mourning, and a garment of praise instead of a spirit of despair. They will be called oaks of righteousness, a planting of the LORD for the display of his splendor.

—Is. 61:1–3

---

[21] Grand Rapids, MI: Chosen Books, 2009.

I have given you authority to trample on snakes and scorpions and to overcome all the power of the enemy; nothing will harm you.

—Luke 10:19

Steps of Deliverance Prayer

1. Preparation

    a. Prayers of protection

    b. Establish a spiritually clean, welcoming environment when possible

    c. Have a team of at least two people to pray, with one clear leader determined

    d. Know the lines of authority (including mandated reporting, guidance for where to go if you need assistance). If you know in advance that the sickness you are praying for is demonic in nature, particularly if the person seeking prayer has a history in the occult, it is best practice to notify your pastor, priest, or spiritual authority, so they can also be in intercession for you and be on hand if further counsel or ministry is needed.

    e. Ask the three permissions[22]
    Note: Sometimes, it is best not to make physical contact while praying for deliverance. However, still establish permission first.

2. Interview

    a. Listen to the Holy Spirit for areas of insight

        i. "God, what are you doing right now?"

        ii. "Is this a good candidate for ministry?"

    b. Listen to the person and ask questions such as:

        i. Why has this person come?

        ii. Are they ready to surrender?
        Note: God will never deliver you from a friend!

---

[22] See Kingdom Lesson 2, The Interview, Step 3: Pray, pages 14–15.

c. Consider: Are there any spiritual obstacles? (Occult activity, curses)

d. Is there a need for repentance? Often, people re-name or rationalize sin, even though they really do want to be free. It's important to realize that sexual sins produce soul-ties, and these must be broken.

3. Summarize

   a. **Repeat back** what you have heard, what you understand, and share any insights from the Holy Spirit or your intuition.
   Note: While the interview may be simple if you know the person well or if the person is well acquainted with his/her needs, be careful not to fall into the trap of overfamiliarity and failing to depend on the Holy Spirit.

   b. **Verbalize how you would like to proceed**. Then, proceed with the person's permission.

   Example: "Let's begin to pray. First, let's ask Jesus to set you free. Then, I'd like to lead you in a prayer of repentance and renunciation (and/or forgiveness). Are you comfortable with this? You can simply repeat after me, and I will pray based on what you have shared and where I feel the Holy Spirit may be leading. If there is anything you disagree with, please tell me—only pray what is true for you. If you prefer to say anything in your own words, please feel free to do so. After I start us off, you can continue as you feel led."

4. Pray

   a. **Renounce**
   The person receiving prayer must renounce each area of bondage in the name of Jesus; the person must verbalize them him/herself. Don't attempt to cast out spirits until they're all renounced. This helps keep manifestations to a minimum.

   b. After each spirit is renounced, **break the power of the spirit in Jesus' name**.
   "I break the bondage of fear in the name of Jesus."

   c. **Take authority**
   "In the name of Jesus, I break the power of every spirit that [name] has

renounced and any related spirit, and I command them to leave now and go straight to the feet of Jesus."

5. Ask

   a. Get feedback
   "How are you feeling? Are any thoughts or emotions surfacing for you?"

   b. Do not tell people that they are free
   That is for them to determine and bear witness to.

   c. If more pain surfaces or old bondage persists, consider repeating the process beginning with more interview questions.

   d. Allow for time!

6. Thanksgiving, blessings, infilling

   a. "Thank you, Jesus, for setting me free from the spirit of [...]." "Thank you, Jesus, that I have forgiven my father for shaming me." If the person is not yet free, suggesting that they thank God will often expose the afflicting spirit. This is a good time to see if there might be an unaddressed root. If there is, repeat the process as necessary: repent, renounce, forgive, etc.

   b. Pray for a fresh (or first) infilling of the Holy Spirit.

   c. Speak words of affirmation and blessing.

   d. Fill the void where the enemy has resided with the spirit of Jesus.

   e. Give parting instructions.

You may want to encourage them to get involved in a small group, advise cleansing their homes of anything representing the kingdom of darkness, or destroy occult items. Offer encouragement or instructions which might assist them in walking out their freedom.

Understanding Manifestations

1. Manifestations can be caused by multiple factors, not all of which are demonic. Seek to understand the cause of any manifestation which arises by asking questions and listening to the Holy Spirit.

2. The enemy seeks to distract, humiliate, and dehumanize. If a person is displaying physical manifestations that are demonic in nature, such as sudden extreme pain, altered voice or consciousness, or humiliating, intimidating, or dehumanizing symptoms, take authority firmly in the name of Jesus. Command the spirit to be silent and cease manifesting.

3. Act immediately on the authority you have taken. Help the person receiving prayer regain control of themselves. Encourage them to look you in the eyes, and use the name of the person receiving ministry.
   "Alice, take control of your body and mind in the name of Jesus. Open your eyes."

4. Interact with the person, not the demonic.

5. Ask for feedback, such as what the individual is feeling at that moment or any thoughts or memories that are coming to mind.

6. Continue to seek clarity and understanding.

Some denominations require contacting a pastor, priest, or bishop when the verifiable need for deliverance or exorcism arises. Be sure to know how best to proceed, given your own church affiliation or the affiliation of the group that you are ministering with.

Notes

KINGDOM LESSON 6

Physical Sickness

*Veiled in flesh the Godhead see,
Hail! The incarnate deity!
Pleased as man with men to dwell;
Jesus, our Emmanuel.*

—*Charles Wesley,
Traditional English Carol, 1739*

*Surely he took up our pain and bore our suffering,
yet we considered him punished by God,
stricken by him, and afflicted.*

—*Isa. 53:4*

Why Do Bodies Matter?

1. Bodies are created by God, and He said they are "very good."

2. Bodies were not originally created to die.

3. That Jesus has a body forever displays the Godhead's commitment to physical bodies.

4. Jesus emphasized the healing of physical bodies throughout his earthly ministry.

5. Physical bodies will be resurrected at the end of this age when all things are made new.

Common False Perceptions About the Human Body

1. Bodies are irrelevant. They're going to die anyway.

2. Human bodies (and all physical matter) are far less important to Christianity than human spirits.

3. Bodies are completely distinct from the mind, will, spirit, and emotions. There is a non-porous separation between the body and the spirit.

4. How you feel determines who you are and has nothing (or very little) to do with your physical body or being created in the image of God.

5. Bodies are actually evil: bodily needs and desires completely or nearly completely corrupt the body, leaving the body only as a source of temptation (to gluttony, laziness, lust, violence, self-hatred, etc.).

What is a Sacrament, and What Makes Matter "Sacramental"?

1. Jesus took what might seem like some significant risks in His use of physical objects (as well as His own body) to be a conduit of the healing power of God. But this practice was not exceptional. Rather, it was in complete harmony with how God had always interacted with His people as physical and spiritual people in a physical and spiritual world.

   What, then, was the remarkable thing that the Twelve Disciples learned as they watched the Divine Healer? This first: that instead of healing them all by a word, instead of willing cures by the wholesale, He took His patients one by one. And then, second—and we need to fix our attention upon it—that as each individual came to Him for treatment, He always made use of material things in effecting His cures… Now it is the common clay; now the water of Siloam; now His own body; His hands; the saliva from His lips, even His garments….

   …Why did He do it that way? We can think of but one answer. His purpose was to accustom the disciples to the use of material things in the conveying of physical gifts of healing, till at length they could grasp the thought of material things in the conveying of spiritual gifts. In other words, He was preparing them for a great principle of the Christian religion, viz., the 'sacramental prin-

ciple', that grace is conveyed to the soul 'through channels'. The things of earth are used to bring men the fights of heaven. Through things visible we are brought to an appreciation of things invisible.[23]

2. Sacramental theology

   a. All of creation was intended to be a conduit of the presence and knowledge of God.

   b. At the Fall, a great divide took place. The body and soul were separated by death, each human from other humans by suspicion and enmity, and humans from God. The sacramental nature of the created order was rent.

   c. In his book *For the Life of the World*, Alexander Schmemann states: "The only real fall of man is his non-Eucharistic life in a non-Eucharistic world. The fall is not that he preferred the world to God, distorted the balance between the spiritual and material, but that he made the world material, whereas he was to have transformed it into 'life in God', filled with meaning and spirit."[24]

   d. Being fully God and fully human, Jesus began in his body the work of restoring all things to eucharistic (thanksgiving) communion with the Godhead. Jesus was and is the ultimate sacrament. The Apostle Paul teaches that this restoring of communion, which can also be seen as the bringing together of heaven and earth, will continue until everything is brought to full unity under Christ at his return (Eph. 1:3–10).

The Healing Ministry of Jesus

1. Jesus used healing during his earthly ministry as the number one illustration of the in-breaking of the Kingdom of Heaven.

2. Jesus disassociated the Jewish assumption that there was always a connection between intentional sin and sickness. However, there were occasions where He either associated the two or used healing as His proof of choice that a person's sins had been forgiven (see Mark 2, the healing of the paralytic.)

---

[23] See Appendix B, pp. 74-75, "The Good Physician," by Charles Fiske.

[24] Alexander Schmemann, *For the Life of the World* (St. Vladimir's Seminary Press, 1997), 18.

3. The Gospels contain 26 accounts of the physical healing of individuals. Remember, too, that large crowds came to Jesus, and "he healed them all" (Matt 8:16).[25]

The Role of Faith in Healing Prayer

1. When asked, Jesus never refused to pray for a sick person. Asking itself is a gesture of humility and faith.

2. Jesus praised the Roman centurion's faith in Matthew 8:5-13. Three characteristics mark his faith:

   a. Humility

   b. Belief in Jesus' authority over creation

   c. Belief in the power of Jesus' word.
   "Faith is the medium through which God releases his healing power. Most divine healing comes as a result of someone's faith in God. After healing someone, Jesus frequently said, "your faith has healed you."[26]

3. Faith can come through different avenues:

   a. The one receiving prayer (see Paul in Lystra, Acts 14:9–10);

   b. Friends and relatives (see the centurion's servant, Jairus' daughter, and the paralytic lowered through the roof);

   c. The one praying for healing.

Note that our faith is weak and broken. Fortunately, our faith is not in our faith but in God's character. Our faith is built as we grow in our understanding of God's character, as well as our intimacy with him.

Patience, Compassion, and Authority

1. Most healings in the New Testament took place immediately, but not all (see Mark 8:22–26 when Jesus heals the blind man in degrees). Francis MacNutt has said:

---

[25] John Wimber, *Power Healing* (San Francisco: Harper and Row), 1987.

[26] Wimber, 141.

> *One of the great discoveries in my life has been that when a short prayer doesn't seem to help, a "soaking" prayer often brings the healing we are looking for. Over and over I have checked the effect of prayer by asking groups how many were totally healed when we prayed a short prayer and how many were improved. The number of people who experience some real improvement usually outnumbers those who are totally healed by five to one. This led me to realize that a short prayer usually has some physical effect (and always a spiritual effect) upon a person, but that most of us need more time when we pray for the sick.*[27]

2. Much physical healing takes place as a part of a process of healing because physical pain and illness are often the result of several factors (emotional, demonic, etc.)

3. It is important that we cultivate a culture of honest, grateful stewardship of the small things. Keep in mind that Jesus taught that the Kingdom of God often grows like a seed (Mk 4:26–9; 30–32) or like yeast in bread dough (Mt 13:33–7), rather than instantaneously. It can be tempting to consider slow growth and healing a "coincidence" rather than miraculous simply because it is taking time. In reality, fast or slow, all healing and life come from God.

Not Everyone Is Healed

1. There is a scriptural precedent for people not being healed.

   Consider the cases of Paul, Timothy (1 Tim. 5:23), Trophimus (1 Tim. 4:20), and Epaphroditus.

2. There are many reasons that people are not healed when prayed for. Some include:

   a. Some people do not have faith for healing (Jas. 5:15);

   b. Personal, unconfessed sin creates a barrier to God's grace (Jas. 5:16);

---

[27] Francis MacNutt, as quoted in Marion Stroud's *Face to Face with Cancer* (Lion Hudson: Oxford, 2004), 154.

    c. Persistent and widespread disunity, sin, and unbelief in bodies of believers and families can inhibit healing in individual members of the body (1 Cor. 11:30);

    d. Because of incomplete or incorrect diagnoses of what is causing their problems, people do not know how to pray correctly;

    e. Some people assume God always heals instantly, and when he does not heal immediately, they stop praying.[28]

3. The "Already Not Yet"

    a. Luke 11 and Luke 18 serve as models for persistence in prayer.

    b. "Our standard of faith and prayer for healing is not our present experience. Our standard is God's heart, which is full of grace and compassion."[29]

FOR FURTHER READING

For a more in-depth look at why people are not healed, Francis MacNutt's *Healing* (1974) contains an excellent chapter on the subject.[30]

---

[28] Wimber, 152.

[29] Wimber, 159.

[30] Francis MacNutt, *Healing* (1999). See Chapter 17, pages 193–204.

Notes

KINGDOM LESSON 7

Hearing the Voice of God for Ministry

Most people would seek the gift [of prophecy] if they understood how much Jesus wants to bless His people by the power of the Spirit. He wants to speak His word into our hearts and affirm our identity in Him... prophetic blessing speaks deep into a person's heart. God knows my name. He knows who I am; He understands me like no other. Encouragement comes because God speaks to the meaning and purpose of my life.

—Neil Lozano, Unbound

Fear not, for I have redeemed you; I have summoned you by name, you are mine.

—Isa. 43:1

FIRST, WHAT IS PROPHECY? For our purposes in this course, prophecy refers to information received supernaturally, communicated to us by the Holy Spirit.

Characteristics of Prophecy

1. Prophecy may include:

    a. Foretelling: Knowledge and communication of events before they happen

    b. Forthtelling: Timely understanding of the purposes and/or heart of God in current events, or for certain people; also, the declaration of the scriptures, the character, and nature of God in an inspired way, which communicates to the heart;

    c. Encouragement, exhortation, building up, comfort, direction, warning (1 Cor. 14:3, Acts 11:27–30, Is 40:1–2, Is. 30:21, Matt 23:37–39). It is often prophetic insight or things like sympathetic pain (when the Holy Spirit causes our own bodies and hearts to resonate with the physical or emotional pain of another person) which help to guide us as we pray for the sick.

2. Prophecy is the testimony of Jesus. All genuine prophetic ministry will:

    a. Point us toward Jesus

    b. Be in agreement with His character and nature as revealed in the scriptures. It will always bear witness to Jesus; who He is, what He is like, how He sees us, and how He feels about us.

At this I fell at his feet to worship him. But he said to me, "Don't do that! I am a fellow servant with you and with your brothers and sisters who hold to the testimony of Jesus. Worship God! For it is the Spirit of prophecy who bears testimony to Jesus."

—Rev. 19:9–11

3. Prophecy is a gift of the Holy Spirit for the church.

Now to each one the manifestation of the Spirit is given for the common good. To one there is given through the Spirit a message of wisdom, to another a message of knowledge by means of the same Spirit, to another faith by the same Spirit, to another gifts of healing by that one Spirit, to another miraculous powers, to another prophecy, to another distinguishing between spirits, to another speaking in different kinds of tongues, and to still another the interpretation of tongues. All these are the work of one and the same Spirit, and he distributes them to each one, just as he determines.

—1 Cor. 12:7–11

Prophecy is a manifestation of the imminence of God: "The Lord is near to all who call on him, to all who call on him in truth" (Psalm 145:18). Through prophetic ministry, we experience what God is like toward us and how He sees us.

Who Can Hear the Voice of God for Ministry?

Potentially, everybody can hear the voice of God for ministry.

> *And it shall come to pass in the last days, says God, that I will pour out of My Spirit on all flesh; your sons and your daughters shall prophesy; your young men shall see visions, your old men shall dream dreams. And on My menservants and on My maidservants I will pour out My Spirit in those days; and they shall prophesy.*
>
> *—Acts 2:17–18*

Prophetic unction is the Holy Spirit sharing with us what is on God's heart for ourselves and others, and the Holy Spirit speaks uniquely to different members of the body of Christ. There will be some people who operate through different manifestations of the gift of prophecy (see again 1 Cor. 12). Those who ask to hear the voice of God will hear. Paul exhorts us to pray for the gift of prophecy. There is often a quantitative relationship between what we are operating in (gifts) and what we are asking for (intercession, intimacy with Jesus).

> *Follow the way of love and eagerly desire gifts of the Spirit, especially prophecy. For anyone who speaks in a tongue does not speak to people but to God. Indeed, no one understands them, they utter mysteries by the Spirit. But the one who prophesies speaks to people for their strengthening, encouraging and comfort. Anyone who speaks in a tongue edifies themselves, but the one who prophesies edifies the church. I would like every one of you to speak in tongues, but I would rather have you prophesy.*
>
> *—1 Cor. 14:1–5a*

Who Is a Prophetic Minister?

In the same way that everyone can share the gospel with their neighbors, but some are particularly gifted and "called" evangelists, and everyone can share what knowledge of God they have, and yet some are gifted and recognized by the church as teachers, there are also individuals anointed by God to function primarily as prophetic ministers within the church. These are men and women particularly gifted by the Holy Spirit, who have been recognized and blessed by the church to serve in this way. Not all people who prophesy (who hear from God and share what they hear with others) are—or should be—recognized by the church as prophetic ministers.

> The greater the potential repercussions of a ministry, the greater the accountability and discernment is needed. We encourage everyone who has not been specifically recognized by their church as a prophetic minister of some kind (and therefore held accountable by that church family or system) to focus on encouragement and building up through prophetic ministry. Rebuke and direction, because they have greater repercussions for individuals and communities, should be carefully discerned by wise members of the church body. This doesn't mean that we cease to be clear about sin, but it does mean that we handle with great care (i.e., with discernment and accountability) words that we believe to be from God, which may have a significant impact on people's lives, their understanding of what God is like, and their decisions.

And God has placed in the church first of all apostles, second prophets, third teachers, then miracles, then gifts of healing, of helping, of guidance, and of different kinds of tongues.

—*1 Cor. 12:28*

Some individuals are recognized specifically as prophets in the Old Testament: Abraham (Gen. 20:7); Moses (Deut. 34:10); Miriam (Exod. 15:20); Deborah (Judges 4:4); Samuel (1 Sam. 3:19-20); David (Acts 2:30); Elijah, Elisha, Hosea, Isaiah, Jeremiah, Ezekiel, Micah, etc. There are also recognized prophets of the New Testament, including Anna (Luke 2:36), John the Baptist (Matt. 11:9-14), Phillip's four daughters (Acts 21:8-9), and Ananias of Damascus (Acts 9:10–18).

Why Bother to Prophesy?

Prophesying is considered one of the crucial ways that we walk out "the way of love" by the Holy Spirit. First Corinthians 14:1 states: "Follow the way of love and eagerly desire gifts of the Spirit, especially prophecy." And 1 Corinthians 12:31 states: "Now eagerly desire the greater gifts." The New Living Translation refers to them as "the most helpful gifts."

Often we are dismissive about this later passage, taking it to be damning by small praise the usefulness of tongue-speaking. However, Paul is not deriding the *gift of the Spirit* which is tongues. He is, in fact, emphasizing the importance of prophecy to the church and the world.

How Do I Hear From God for the Purposes of Ministry?

1. **Listen.** We must begin with a heart posture of listening. In general, we like to be heard more than we like to hear. From the time we are children, we seek to make our voices heard. Knowing that what we think and feel and how we express our thoughts and feelings matters to those close to us establishes much of our sense of self-worth. For some of us, this process was stunted by rejection or deprivation, and finding our voices is an expression of "true self" and part of our own healing process. It is from that place of security, however, that we begin the journey into Christian listening. Developing a listening heart is a process, and we practice and grow in listening in many ways, including:

    a. Scripture reading
    The primary way that we learn the heart and language of the Father is through reading the scriptures. And not in reading only, but in believing that the Word is alive—that God Himself is speaking to us when we are not simply passive observers of scripture, but recipients on an intentional heart level. (See Paul's prayer for the Ephesians, in chapter 1:17–19.)

    b. Listening prayer

    c. Practicing loving attentiveness to God throughout the day

    d. Stepping out in faith
    Often we grow by doing and in the process of practicing, rather than in waiting alone.

2. **Spend time with other people who make it a practice of listening to God for the purpose of ministry.** Much of this kind of ministry is better caught than taught.

3. **Believe.** Jesus stated in John 10:

    > *Very truly I tell you Pharisees, anyone who does not enter the sheep pen by the gate, but climbs in by some other way, is a thief and a robber. The one who enters by the gate is the shepherd of the sheep. The gatekeeper opens the gate for him, and the sheep listen to his voice. He calls his own sheep by name and leads them out. When he has brought out all his own, he goes on ahead of them, and his sheep follow him because they know his voice.*

We must believe that he is the good shepherd and that his sheep know his voice. If you are a born-again follower of Jesus, you can hear His voice.

> *If you love me, keep my commands. And I will ask the Father, and he will give you another advocate to help you and be with you forever— the Spirit of truth. The world cannot accept him, because it neither sees him nor knows him. But you know him, for he lives with you and will be in you. I will not leave you as orphans; I will come to you. Before long, the world will not see me anymore, but you will see me. Because I live, you also will live. On that day you will realize that I am in my Father, and you are in me, and I am in you. Whoever has my commands and keeps them is the one who loves me. The one who loves me will be loved by my Father, and I too will love them and show myself to them.*
>
> —*John 14:15–21*

Show[31] in this passage is a translation of the Greek word *emphanizo*, meaning: "To manifest, exhibit to view, to show oneself, come to view, appear, indicate, disclose, declare, make known."[32] We can be confident that we are His own and that He manifests Himself to us.

What does the voice of the Holy Spirit sound like toward us? "But the fruit of the Spirit is love, joy, peace, forbearance, kindness, goodness, faithfulness, gentleness and self-control" (Gal. 5:22–23).

4. **Ask.** And go on asking, believing that often the Kingdom of God grows like seeds in the ground, rather than instant adulthood and full manifestation. Consider James 4:2, "You do not have because you do not ask," and 1 Corinthians 14:1, "Follow the way of love and eagerly desire gifts of the Spirit, especially prophecy."

    a. We ask for guidance: "Holy Spirit, what are you saying/doing here? Now?"

    b. We ask for power: "Holy Spirit, release your power in me."

Learn how to respectfully give voice to the impressions you receive. Often, God gives us more as we respond to His promptings in faith.

---

[31] "Show," *Strong's Exhaustive Concordance: New American Standard Bible*, updated ed., Lockman Foundation, 1995. *Bible Study Tools Online*, www.biblestudytools.com/concordances/strongs-exhaustive-concordance/1718

[32] Thayer's Greek Lexicon, Electronic Database, 2011.

Hindrances to Hearing God:

1. **Earth-bound wisdom:**

   When we view a person, situation, or event through the lens of our own wisdom and understanding without standing in the councils of God, we can hinder our ability to hear. Earth-bound wisdom prevents us from hearing and believing true words of prophecy and traps us in easy, popular, or even outright incorrect judgments. Wisdom and understanding only informed by our own experience are often incompatible with our identity as the new creation. There are many scriptural examples of prophets tripped up by earth-bound wisdom.

   a. The prophet Samuel, sent by God to anoint the new king of Israel:

   > *When they arrived, Samuel saw Eliab and thought, "Surely the Lord's anointed stands here before the Lord." But the Lord said to Samuel, "Do not consider his appearance or his height, for I have rejected him. The Lord does not look at the things people look at. People look at the outward appearance, but the Lord looks at the heart.*

   > —1 Sam. 16:6–7

   b. Eli, observing Hannah praying in the temple:

   > *It so happened that as she continued in prayer before God, Eli was watching her closely. Hannah was praying in her heart, silently. Her lips moved, but no sound was heard. Eli jumped to the conclusion that she was drunk. He approached her and said, "You're drunk! How long do you plan to keep this up? Sober up, woman!" Hannah said, "Oh no, sir—please! I'm a woman brokenhearted. I haven't been drinking. Not a drop of wine or beer. The only thing I've been pouring out is my heart, pouring it out to God. Don't for a minute think I'm a bad woman. It's because I'm so desperately unhappy and in such pain that I've stayed here so long.*

   > —1 Sam. 1:1–16

   c. Zachariah, the father of John the Baptist, had difficulty accepting the words of prophecy from the angel Gabriel about his wife conceiving a child due to his reliance on his own understanding ("We're too old to conceive"), rather than the councils of God (Luke 1:11–20).

   d. Peter, having a vision regarding God's acceptance of the Gentiles, did not rationally understand what God was getting at and argued with God:

> *About noon the following day as they were on their journey and approaching the city, Peter went up on the roof to pray. He became hungry and wanted something to eat, and while the meal was being prepared, he fell into a trance. He saw heaven opened and something like a large sheet being let down to earth by its four corners. It contained all kinds of four-footed animals, as well as reptiles and birds. Then a voice told him, 'Get up, Peter. Kill and eat.' 'Surely not, Lord!' Peter replied. 'I have never eaten anything impure or unclean.' The voice spoke to him a second time, "Do not call anything impure that God has made clean. This happened three times, and immediately the sheet was taken back to heaven.*
>
> —Acts 10:9–16

2. **Believing that we are not meant to hear from God or are not the kind of people who can hear God.**

   Unfortunately, many of us are not growing in confidence that we are able to hear God and can grow in our ability to hear. We are waiting for an audible voice from Heaven or some sort of Holy Spirit in-breaking for God to prove to us that we are capable of hearing Him and that He actually wants to speak to (and through) us. In reality, this is often born of subtle testing of God, reminiscent of the Devil's temptation of Jesus in the wilderness: "If you are really the Son of God…". It is as though we are saying something to the effect of "If I am really clean enough to use as a vessel for your word," or "If you really want to say something to me, you will prove yourself by…". In reality, we have been made clean by the blood of Jesus and will never be more righteous than we were when we first believed. Additionally, He has promised to make Himself known to us.

3. **Personal sin, particularly judgment, prevents us from spiritually hearing, seeing, and understanding clearly.**

   > *Do not judge, or you too will be judged. For in the same way you judge others, you will be judged, and with the measure you use, it will be measured to you. Why do you look at the speck of sawdust in your brother's eye and pay no attention to the plank in your own eye? How can you say to your brother, "Let me take the speck out of your eye," when all the time there is a plank in your own eye? You hypocrite, first take the plank out of your own eye, and then you will see clearly to remove the speck from your brother's eye.*
   >
   > —Matt. 7:1–5

4. **Fear: of failure, of looking foolish, of God not showing up.**

Four Ways of Hearing

Consider the following four ways people may often hear or see what the Father is doing in order to engage prophetic ministry, all of which must be subjected to discernment:

1. **Interior Impressions:**
   Often a subtle nudge or sense from the Holy Spirit; interior, inaudible, usually a prompting on the heart. This can happen ahead of time, but the Spirit usually grants these when we are ministering to people.

> God may be gently sharing with us an applicable passage of scripture, encouraging us to reach out in love, or giving us insight into how to continue to pray. Because these impressions are often gentle or subtle, they require clear confirmation. Don't hesitate to ask for clarity from the person for whom you are praying. This can sound something like, "As I am praying for you, _____ is coming to mind. Does this resonate with you, or mean anything helpful to us as we pray?"

2. **Physical Sensations:**
   Physical experiences (sight, sound, smell, taste, touch), which are from the Holy Spirit, and lead us in how to pray for a person or situation. This includes what is sometimes referred to as "sympathetic pain," where God grants the minister understanding of another person's condition or situation through personal experience—the Lord shares with the prayer minister the experience or sensation of a hurting person so that he or she might pray with understanding and faith. The Holy Spirit also sometimes allows us to feel a physical sensation (fire, wind, heat, oil, power, and so on) or a physical/emotional pain (sympathetic pain) that corresponds with how He will touch others.

3. **Visible manifestations of the movement of the Holy Spirit:**
   Tears, flushed face, sweating, trembling, change in breathing patterns.

4. **Dreams and visions:**
   The Holy Spirit may show us what He is doing by giving us a prophetic dream or vision about a person or situation before we minister.[33]

---

[33] Mike Bickle, *Growing in the Prophetic* (Lake Mary, FL: Charisma House, 1996, 2008); 173.

False Equations Regarding Prophetic Ministry

1. Character equals anointing (the idea that spiritual gifting endorses character or character produces spiritual gifts).

2. Anointing, or visible success in ministry, equals divine endorsement of ministry style.

3. Anointing equals 100% accuracy.

Of course, none of these are true.

Another false belief is that prophetic ministers are not subject to the same standards of decency, growth, maturity, and accountability within the church.

If I believe God has shared something with me, I might think I automatically have permission to act immediately, and however I would like, rather than submitting what I believe I am hearing or seeing to my spiritual authorities.[34] This is false.

The process of receiving, discerning, and applying what God share is just that: a process. And it is a process that best takes place within a community, utilizing the various giftings and leadership available as we grow in love, and in fellowship with one another.

Conclusion

> *Then Jesus came to them and said, "All authority in Heaven and on Earth has been given to me. Therefore go and make disciples of all nations, baptizing them in the name of the Father and of the Son and of the Holy Spirit, and teaching them to obey everything I have commanded you. And surely I am with you always, to the very end of the age."*
>
> —*Matthew 28:18–20*

In Matthew chapter 28, Jesus exhorts His disciples a final time before ascending into Heaven. His parting instructions to His dear friends and followers are to be their great mission statement, styled by the church in the years to come as "the Great Commission." It was Jesus' plan all along to teach renewed

---

[34] Bickle, 105-111.

humanity a way to be conduits of renewal, as He sent them out to make disciples in the only way they knew how—the way in which He had discipled them. It is my great hope in this manual that we are re-called to the way in which Jesus made disciples: He taught them not only truths to live by, but He also gifted them with the power, through the Holy Spirit, to demonstrate truth and to advance His Kingdom with power and love, words and deeds. It is my prayer that we would pray with confidence and increasing skill and zeal "Thy Kingdom come, Thy will be done, on Earth as it is in Heaven," until that great day when Heaven and Earth are finally and completely united, and the old order of sin, sickness and death finally and fully pass away.

A series of appendices have been included at the end of this manual as supplemental learning material, as well as a closer look at a few topics which may be helpful as you and your community pray for the sick and hurting.

May God the Father, the Son, and the Holy Spirit fill you, and bless you, and grant you great courage, power, and hope as you go into the world to declare with word and deed the coming Kingdom.

Notes

APPENDIX A

Key Scriptures

Isaiah 61:1-3

¹The Spirit of the Sovereign Lord is on me, because the Lord has anointed me to proclaim good news to the poor. He has sent me to bind up the brokenhearted, to proclaim freedom for the captives and release from darkness for the prisoners,

²to proclaim the year of the Lord's favor and the day of vengeance of our God, to comfort all who mourn,

³and provide for those who grieve in Zion— to bestow on them a crown of beauty instead of ashes,

> the oil of joy
> instead of mourning,
> and a garment of praise
> instead of a spirit of despair.

They will be called oaks of righteousness, a planting of the Lord for the display of his splendor.

Luke 4:14-21

¹⁴Jesus returned to Galilee in the power of the Spirit, and news about him spread through the whole countryside. 15He was teaching in their synagogues, and everyone praised him.

¹⁶He went to Nazareth, where he had been brought up, and on the Sabbath day he went into the synagogue, as was his custom. He stood up to read, ¹⁷and the scroll of the prophet Isaiah was handed to him. Unrolling it, he found the place where it is written:

¹⁸"The Spirit of the Lord is on me,
  because he has anointed me
  to proclaim good news to the poor.

He has sent me to proclaim freedom for the prisoners
and recovery of sight for the blind,
to set the oppressed free,
¹⁹to proclaim the year of the Lord's favor."

²⁰Then he rolled up the scroll, gave it back to the attendant and sat down. The eyes of everyone in the synagogue were fastened on him. 21 He began by saying to them, "Today this scripture is fulfilled in your hearing."

John 20:19-23

¹⁹On the evening of that first day of the week, when the disciples were together, with the doors locked for fear of the Jewish leaders, Jesus came and stood among them and said, "Peace be with you!" ²⁰After he said this, he showed them his hands and side. The disciples were overjoyed when they saw the Lord. ²¹Again Jesus said, "Peace be with you! As the Father has sent me, I am sending you." ²²And with that he breathed on them and said, "Receive the Holy Spirit. ²³If you forgive anyone's sins, their sins are forgiven; if you do not forgive them, they are not forgiven."

APPENDIX B

The Good Physician
By Charles Fiske[35]

JESUS CHRIST was the Good Physician. Even those who stumble at the other miracles of the Bible, believe in the Gospel stories of Christ's healing power, however they explain the facts. The records of His gracious deeds run so closely through the narrative that they are like threads woven into the cloth from which cannot be cut out without destroying the garment.

The picture is plain. Jesus Christ went about through the fields and hills of Galilee restoring into harmony with the beautiful world about Him the disease-laden bodies of the multitudes of sick folk who came to see Him. He was first known as the Healer.

The Good Physician had a company of pupils who watched Him at His work. He was like a surgeon in a clinic, with the eyes of his students fixed upon him. Everywhere the little company of His disciples went with Him on His errands of mercy. Because of their presence He seemed to hold himself in. He did only what an overflowing pity compelled Him to do; and He did it in such a way as to teach while He worked. He wanted to instruct that little band of followers and make them understand His method and see its significance.

As the tide of patients swept in upon Him the disciples noticed a strange thing about the Master's work of healing. They had come to believe that all power was given Him, and yet He exercised that power only within limitations. They had

---

[35] Fiske, Charles. "The Good Physician," in *Back to Christ: The Wonder of His Life, the Romance of His Religion, Forgotten Truths of His Teaching, Some Practical Applications of His Gospel* (New York: Longmans, Green and Co., 1917), 30-40.

come to believe that He could heal by a word; yet with the crowds pressing Him He chose a slower, plodding way.

For the multitudes did indeed besiege Him from every side. The demands upon His skill spread like a conflagration. Half the countryside flung themselves upon His vitality and sympathy. His patients were of all classes, all disorders, all shades of faith, all varieties of gratitude and ingratitude. They crowded around Him till He hardly had time to eat or to sleep. So they came and so they were healed.

What, then, was the remarkable thing the Twelve Disciples learned as they watched the Divine Healer? This first: That instead of healing them all by a word, instead of willing cures by the wholesale, He took His patients one by one. And then, second – and we need to fix our attention upon it – that that as each individual came to Him for treatment, He always made use of material things in effecting his cures.

Remember that the apostles believed in His power to heal; believed that He might have healed all who came by the simple exercise of that power, without any assistance from without. What must have been their thoughts when they saw how He chose to work? Some material object seemed always to be the medium through which the healing was effected. Now it is the common clay; now the waters of Siloam; now His own body; His hands; the saliva from His lips; even His garments. There was a man born deaf and with an impediment in his speech; Jesus took him aside from the multitude, put His fingers in the man's ears, touched his tongue. A blind man came to see Him: He spat on the ground, made clay of the spittle, anointed his eyes and sent him to the pool to wash. Out of all the recorded miracles of healing there are only five which were not accompanied by the use of some material object or physical agency; and in each of these cases there is a special reason for the variation from His customary method. Usually, ordinarily, He used material helps; and of the numerous other miraculous cures of which there is no detailed record, it is said that "He laid His hands upon them and healed them every one."

Now mark. He did this in spite of the apparent peril of arousing among the people a dangerous superstition. We know how easy it is for ignorant people to attribute a cure to some special object. Pilgrimages to the shrines of saints are not unknown to-day, and many cures have been attributed to the virtue of holy relics.

Appendix B: The Good Physician

There was always that danger when Jesus the Good Physician wrought His cures: the danger that instead of attention being fixed upon Himself alone, it might be fixed upon the things He used, and the cure be attributed to some healing quality of the particular clay or water; it might be supposed that there was virtue in the touch of His garment; men's minds might be directed away from the Healer; they might forget Him and remember only the material He employed.

Why, then, did He persist in His method? Must not the apostles have asked that question again and again? What did He mean? There they were, students in the clinic, watching the Master at His work, feeling that He wanted their attention, and that He had some purpose in arousing their questioning. Why did He do it in that way?

We can think of but one answer. His purpose was to accustom the disciples to the use of material things in the conveying of physical gifts of healing, till at length they could grasp the thought that in the same way He meant to make use of material things in the conveying of spiritual gifts. In other words, He was preparing them for a great principle of the Christian religion, viz., the sacramental principle, that grace is conveyed to the soul "through channels." The things of earth are used to bring to men the gifts of heaven. Through things visible we are brought to an appreciation of things invisible.

So as they question in their hearts, He speaks to them by and by of baptism; He tells Nicodemus that one must be born again of water and the Spirit.; at the close of His ministry He sends out His disciples to administer baptismal grace in the name of the Father, and of the Son, and of the Holy Spirit. Again He tells them that their life must be fed from Him; that except they eat the flesh of the Son of Man and drink His blood, they have no life in them; and when there has been time for the thought to sink into their minds He takes bread and wine, blesses it and tells them that this is the Body and Blood of which He has spoken. When the day comes that He ordains them to send them forth as the Father had sent Him, He lays His hands upon them and breathes on them, that in the very act their faith may be stimulated to believe in the fact of inflowing grace.

Here then we have the source of the sacramental system: Christ Himself. He it is, and no one else, who ordains that spiritual grace shall come through material channels: the water of baptism a laver of inward spiritual purification; the bread and wine of Holy Communion the mystical means of imparting the life of Christ; the laying on of hands as the appointed method of the coming of the Spirit of strength and comfort; all outward and visible signs of an inward and spiritual grace given us.

Sometimes men have objected to the Church's insistence on the sacraments as though sacraments were substitutes for individual devotion to Jesus Christ, ceremonies and forms that smother personal piety, something to bring the Church and the clergy between the soul and God and hindering union with Christ. Of course it is not in this way that the Church preaches the sacramental principle. Church doctrine, after all, is Bible truth. Sacraments are really Christ's appointed means of union with Himself; blessed channels of grace by which love may be fed and union with God made perfect and devotion to Him kept alive. "Back to Christ," we hear men say; back of churches and creeds and sacraments to Jesus Himself. But when we go back to Christ we find ourselves in the very atmosphere of Church teaching. He and He alone is authority for our doctrine. Call the sacramental system absurd, if you will; but remember it originated with the Lord Christ Himself. Whether you understand the need of it or not, it is His method; and when you object to it your objection is not against the Church's plan, it is against Christ's own scheme of salvation.

But why did Jesus Christ establish such a system? Why does He not always give life to the soul without such helps?

We may suggest three reasons.

First. Because it is the simplest way to bring us to a realization of spiritual things. For our sakes grace is brought to us through external channels. We are not disembodied spirits; we are here in the body, with all the drawbacks of a bodily existence. Glimpses of heaven open to us, and then we fall back to earth; the soaring spirit is held down by the flesh. So by Christ's sacramental method, faith is stimulated by sense. As in the miracles of healing the touch of the hand, the finger on the tongue, the clay on the eyes, the water of the pool, aroused the faith of those who were to be healed, made them ready and expectant, helped them to feel that something was being done for them – so now, there is something we can see, touch, taste, handle, that faith may be quickened. The outward symbol is a pledge to assure us of grace given, as well as a means to its reception.

And not only an aid to faith, but a test of faith. It is enough for us that Christ has given the command; the faithful follower obeys, whether he understands or not. It is to be expected that one who submits loyally and obediently to a command or expressed wish of Christ should receive a blessing.

If a man opens his heart wide in loving response to the wish of another, that person's spirit inevitably enters. We see this sacramental act of receiving the spirit of another in every child who obeys, from a glad love, his father or his mother, in every student who tries hard to fulfill his great master's will for him; in every friend who from love tries to please his friend.[36]

Our Lord asks us to seek grace this way. It is a love test and faith test – and we obey. Second. We are souls in bodies, because the body is the expression of the soul's life. We shall always be souls in bodies; in the life of the world to come the soul will have that through which its life is expressed. Therefore the redemption of the soul will be the redemption of the body as well; and it is fitting that the gift to the soul should come through physical channels, so that every part of our nature may share in the bestowal of grace.

Third. Perhaps there is still a deeper purpose. May it not be that all creation is to share in the plan of redemption? St. Paul seems to suggest the fall of man involved the whole created universe, which "groaneth and travaileth in pain," waiting for its redemption and ours. So nature, itself to be redeemed, is made use of in God's redemptive work, as the Holy Spirit, through natural elements exalted to a spiritual efficacy, ministers to the diseases of the soul.

Who can tell how far this thought may carry us? Does it mean that this world, purified and become a scene of unfettered spiritual activity, shall be the new heaven and the new earth of the seer's vision? Does it mean that we have lost something of the romance and poetry of redemption when we forget the mystery of nature in our effort to exalt the mystery of grace? Does it mean that in going back to Christ we have found the source of mystery in each?

It is He who gives nature its beauty and its charm. Back of all that we see is God the Unseen; God and His spiritual hosts. Every pleasing prospect is, as it were, the expression of His presence, the moving of the robes of those whose faces see God.

And back of the sacramental water and the sacramental bread and wine is the same Christ. He charges them with power. He fills them with grace. In Him is the current of life for which they are they conveyors. So we pass from symbols to the

---

[36] Slattery, Charles Lewis, *The Light Within: A Study of the Holy Spirit*, (New York: Longmans, Green and Co., 1915).

thing symbolized, from the outward form to the inward reality; and we talk, trembling yet joyous, in the very presence of God.

Perhaps it may be only a fancy; but it is a beautiful fancy, this thought of a sacramental system. A poet-priest has expressed it more beautifully than any words of ours can put it. He tells how, one Saturday afternoon in midsummer, he stood on the shore of Otsego Lake, looking on: "a scene for which quiet and soothing beauty can hardly be surpassed. Before him lay the mirror of the Glimmerglass; warm lights threw a flush upon the skies; the day was going away; the omens of evening were already in the clouds; the woods were reflected in their native colors along the silent shore. But below was more than what met the eye. Through and under this exterior beauty voices could be heard, speaking of the mystery of the natural world. It has been said of the study of nature that it is hardly profane to characterize it as a means of grace. Here are depths which no man has yet sounded. Whence, and how, came this wondrous, beautiful world; by what bond and to what extent is it so related to man as to sympathize with him in his sorrows and partake of his hope – what poet, what philosopher, what theologian has told us the whole truth on these points?[37]

On the following morning the visitor found himself at an early Eucharistic celebration in the church on the lake. Here another mystery confronted him, like the other too deep to search out; the mystery of the coming of the Lord in Holy Communion.

Both mysteries are of God; one in the order of nature, the other in the order of grace. This lover of nature was a lover of God and as he thought of both he reverently asked many questions. May not the mystery in nature pass onward and upward to the mystery in grace? May there not be relationships between them more intimate than we suppose, too subtle for us to comprehend? And may not this be the true explanation of the sacramental system? May not the mystery in grace be more deeply felt when interpreted by the mystery in nature? At any rate it is the same Hand which beckons to us in both, and in both is stretched out to comfort and bless.

---

[37] Birdsall, Ralph, "The Church," in Fenimore Cooper's *Grave and Christ Churchyard*, (New York: Frederick H. Hitchcock, 1911), 64.

APPENDIX C

Suffering and the Ministry of Healing

–Amy Howard–

THROUGHOUT MY YEARS in healing prayer ministry, one of the most challenging and often neglected conversations I have witnessed coming from pastors and healing ministers is that of suffering well. In communities where supernatural healing is embraced and even pursued, sermons about suffering are rarely heard. And in places that emphasize the growth of character and the sovereignty of God, prayer for healing often takes a back seat, if it happens at all. But for those who choose to live in the tension—that uncomfortable distance between the pain we see and experience and the Kingdom of "thy Kingdom come"—what is there to be said? How do we navigate the distance in time between the "now," where the suffering is, and the future healing for which we pray?

This tension is most readily seen in our own lives, or in the lives of those we care about. It crops up when desires that are out of alignment with God's good and gracious will just won't go away. It appears when our longing for healing collides with the stark reality of death. When God does not readily act in the way that we long for him to, we are left with a deep sense of apparent unfairness, or injustice. Why would God ask us to keep "believing in things hoped for" (Hebrews 11:1) rather than adjust either our behavior or expectations? At least on the one hand, our immediate desires might be satisfied, and on the other, we wouldn't feel continually set up for disappointment.

Suffering well is a theme neglected by Western culture, both outside and within the church today. Speaking as a member of the Millennial generation, I don't know whether anybody quite gets this like we do. We might still love the ideas of nobility, honor, and courage in the face of pain. But we have no confidence in our own ability to be steadfast; no sense that such character and hope have been built into us that we might bear the weight of true suffering to a more glorious end. And from our own fear of our own cowardice, we certainly cannot judge the suffering of others. Who are we to tell somebody else to suffer?

The human condition being what it is, the journey up, out of, and through many kinds of pain often involves a measure of suffering. In his book, *Setting Love in Order,* Mario Bergner wrote poignantly about an evening of suffering early on in his journey into sexual healing.[38] He recalled a Friday night when he found himself utterly alone. Like many people journeying from a realm of broken identity, addiction, or dysfunction, community was essential for him. In the sponsor-sponsee relationship, a phone call is often the lifeline between a despairing dive back into an addictive cycle. For Mario, the nightly meetings and constant community involvement had acted as a buoy in the beginning season of coming to terms with and sorting through the morass of his emotional, spiritual, and physical pain. Berger recounted an evening early on in his journey when he found himself desperately alone. The final meeting for the week had ended Thursday night. After work on Friday, the excruciating hours between the distraction and fellowship of 5:00 Friday to 9:00 Sunday morning stretched before him into an eternity of seconds. He describes his descent into the personal suffering of temptation and aloneness, eventually resorting to taping a band-aid over his door to prevent himself from running to the nearest gay bar. The place of desperate clinging to the cross during those hours was palpable.

The journey to wholeness is often fraught with trial, self-denial, personal failure, and loneliness. No one bears the actual cross but in the place he or she is quite alone, humanly speaking. And lest we be tempted or intimidated by cultural volume to believe these difficulties to be unique to the sexually broken, a good portion of our challenges are found in all boundaries (sexual or otherwise) which

---

[38] Mario Bergner, *Setting Love in Order* (Grand Rapids, MI: Hamewith Books, 1995).

Appendix C: Suffering, Sexuality and the Ministry of Healing

God requires of all people. The pain of aloneness can be acute. It is equally real for the person healing from the constellations of pain permeating from homosexuality as it is for the unmarried college student, the barren couple longing to conceive but continuing to choose monogamy over other culturally available options, and the trauma victim who is choosing to forgive even while inflicted pain continues to echo and reverberate through her heart and body. The reality for those of us who are, in the words of the author of Hebrews, "seeking a better country," is that suffering will come to us all.[39]

I am often surprised afresh by the audacity of St. Peter in his first epistle. St. Peter was writing, we know, to a group of early believers who were in the throes of injustice and suffering. These communities were the victims of the horrific persecutions of Nero. Who can say what it must have been like to live daily on the precipice of humiliation, suffering, loss, and even death for themselves and those they held dear? Certainly not I, a weak and broken, often un-courageous woman in the comfort of my air-conditioned, well-caffeinated Western Christianity. What word would anybody dare bring to such a suffering people? Are we not friends to sufferers at our very best when we are silent but present companions?

And yet. And yet the Apostle, who himself had abdicated the suffering incumbent upon persecution for Jesus' sake, had the nerve to speak, and not only to speak, but to instruct, teach, and encourage those who were suffering the very fate he had at one time thrust aside.[40] And what did he say?

> *Therefore, preparing your minds for action, and being sober-minded, set your hope fully on the grace that will be brought to you at the revelation of Jesus Christ.*
>
> —*1 Pet. 1:13*

There are so many possible pitfalls when it comes to addressing suffering through the lens of the healing ministry. When we suffer, the most natural response is to fix our gaze on the end of that suffering: the healing of illness, the reordering of desire. In and outside the church, we often encourage suffering for the wrong things, creating the idea that God only and ever wants us to suffer. And

---

[39] Heb. 11:14

[40] See Luke 22:55–62.

lastly, those things which, when suffered, have actual potential to unite us with Christ, we often dismiss, avoid, transfer, or reason away.

Suffering well involves seeing suffering through the lens of Christ. There is an ultimate way in which we will be given grace when Christ is finally and fully revealed to all creation. But there is a now-grace when Christ is revealed in our circumstances. This is the crux of the inner healing ministry: to allow for encounter with Christ in the places of our heart wounding, whether trauma, abuse, neglect, or pain. We are constantly inviting Jesus to reveal himself in the physical, psychological, and emotional memories themselves. From that vantage point, our suffering is not just "building character" or "being healed" but forging a reality, an intimacy, and even a friendship with a suffering God.

> *Yet whatever gains I had, these I have come to regard as loss because of Christ. More than that, I regard everything as loss because of the surpassing value of knowing Christ Jesus my Lord. For his sake I have suffered the loss of all things, and I regard them as rubbish, in order that I may gain Christ and be found in him, not having a righteousness of my own that comes from the law, but one that comes through faith in Christ, the righteousness from God based on faith. I want to know Christ and the power of his resurrection and the sharing of his sufferings by becoming like him in his death, if somehow I may attain the resurrection from the dead.*
>
> —Phil. 3:7–11

In the words of Michael Ramsey, Archbishop of Canterbury during the 1960s and 1970s:

> *Like the Christ, the Church is sent to execute a twofold work in the face of the sufferings of men; to seek to alleviate them, to heal them, and to remove them, since they are hateful to God—yet, when they are overwhelming and there is no escape from them, to transfigure them and use them as the raw material of love. So in every age Christians have fought to remove sufferings, and have also borne witness to the truth that they can be transfigured and can become the place where the power of God is known.*[41]

And so it is with the healing ministry as it looks both outwards and inwards at the suffering of sexual and identity brokenness. Our mission is first to minister, love, and pray unto the healing of wounding, forgiveness of sin, reordering of desire, and remaking after the very image of God. Secondly, it is to bear witness to

---

[41] Michael Ramsey, *The Gospel and the Catholic Church* (Peabody, MA: Hendrickson Publishers Marketing, LLC, 2009).

Appendix C: Suffering, Sexuality and the Ministry of Healing

the transforming union with Christ available in the midst of our present suffering. We will, like Peter, encourage ourselves and those to whom we minister to have a "fixed gaze," not on the healing of our present circumstances or sufferings, but on the reality that Jesus is coming, both to these circumstances themselves, and ultimately to the entire Earth itself, when Heaven and Earth are fully united at his physical return, and every last thing that hurts will finally be made new.

There is most certainly a difference between the pursuit of Buddhist Nirvana — the relief of suffering by somehow not feeling it, or our Western solution of medicating, marrying, ignoring, renaming or denying the sources of our pain, and the Christian baptism of suffering into union with a suffering God. Oh, union with the Christ! Is there any one thing that can both ignite and satiate the unmatchable hunger of the human, body and soul? And this is what He offers us if we desire it. This is the invitation for a generation and a culture bending under the weight of suffering, displaced, and hemorrhaging human identity. We will share in the very nature of God if we can only hold still long enough to be loved into being—often in the very places of our deepest wounding.

APPENDIX D

Ministry Styles

Again Jesus said, "Peace be with you! As the Father has sent me, I am sending you." And with that he breathed on them and said, "Receive the Holy Spirit."

—*John 20:21–22*

Then Jesus came to them and said, "All authority in heaven and on earth has been given to me. Therefore go and make disciples of all nations, baptizing them in the name of the Father and of the Son and of the Holy Spirit, and teaching them to obey everything I have commanded you. And surely I am with you always, to the very end of the age."

—*Matthew 28:18–30*

JESUS SPENT THREE YEARS teaching His disciples how to live as citizens and ambassadors of the Kingdom of God. He taught them how to pray, drive out demons, and heal the sick. They ate with Him, traveled with Him, and watched Him interact with those who hated Him, loved Him, wanted to use Him for their own gain, were suspicious of Him, and those who longed for His love. The disciples saw His personality, what He was like when He was hungry and tired. They watched the ways in which Jesus responded to the people He was with—His absolute truth-telling, his patience, and ability to extend both profound challenges as well as invitations. Forty days after His resurrection from the dead, Jesus commissioned His disciples to carry on the work that He had begun in the power of the Holy Spirit. And then He left. From the ascension onwards, all followers of Jesus, empowered and led by the Holy Spirit, would carry on the work that Jesus began. And also like Jesus on earth, they operated within the confines and potentialities of their human bodies, personalities, and relationships.

Let's face it: there are many potential pitfalls to ministering while also being a human. We get strange ideas about what it means to be holy, what it means to minister, how things should look, sound, or feel. Our ministry (read: *love*) can be tainted, distorted, and corrupted by our ambition, immaturity, judgments, and pride. We want to look good, to be received well, and to be seen as spiritual. We are afraid of messing up, and so we refuse to take risks. We are afraid, fragile, or stubborn, and so we become unteachable and therefore unable to experience the joy of real, transformative personal and community growth. We all face these challenges if we attempt to love outwards, practicing the fruits of the Spirit as we mature in our ministry, our ability to hear, respond, be, and love.

Being human and ministering in the power of the Holy Spirit does not mean that we check our humanity at the door and somehow become other than what we are when we pray. But it is an invitation to steadily growing up in love, working toward unity within the Church, and maturity in practice.

Here are a few steps you can take as you journey down the road to becoming the ambassador of the Kingdom you are called to be:

1. Acknowledge where the immaturity or outright sins of other ministers you have seen, heard, or interacted with have hurt you or others you care about. Ask the Lord to show you how these people have impacted you and your attitude, thoughts, and feelings regarding ministering in the power of the Holy Spirit. Take the time to intentionally forgive, and release them from your judgment. You can never truly flourish as an ambassador of love if you are in bondage to judgment or past pain.

2. Exercise patience toward yourself as you grow as a prayer minister. Immaturity is not the same thing as sinfulness—we all must start somewhere. Find a safe person with whom you can process emotions that arise when you step out in faith. Strive to create a culture with clear guidelines and safe policies, and define what risks are acceptable within the setting so people know how and when to step out in faith. Promote a culture of teachability and "failing forward," rebuking strongly only in the face of intentional and repeated rule-breaking.

3. Make love the main thing. When ministering, follow the rules we have come to affectionately refer to as "prophetiquette."

a. Your normal voice will do just fine. Often, increased volume and an urgent or harsh tone can detract from love and produce a feeling of manipulation. So, unless God Himself intervenes, keep it level.

b. Operate at the level of faith you have and within the bounds of responsibility you have been given within your community. God releases authority and faith in His time and as we grow. It is crucial that in hearing from God, we do not respond in a way that unnecessarily divides communities, undermines godly authority, or self-promotes rather than serves.

c. Formulaic approaches to healing ministry don't tend to have great results. Remember, God is out for relationship, not just getting things (such as healing the sick) done. Avoid the tendency toward formulas in healing ministry. Formulaic thinking such as "If I command this sickness, then it will have to leave," or "If I minister such and such a way, I will get the results I want (or have seen in the past)" often has a damaging result. It can produce resentment or shame in both ministers and those to whom they minister when desired results aren't achieved.

d. Unless your ministry has been sanctioned and vetted by your local leadership, avoid words of correction, rebuke, direction, or predictive prophecy (we say, "No dates, mates, or babies"). Allow your ministry to mature as it is tested and strengthened by love.

e. Steer clear of strange words that those you are ministering to may not understand. Ministries often have a culture, and with culture comes common language or jargon, which is completely normal. However, it is important that we aim to be understood by the outsider. We do not want to alienate people with the use of strange phrasing or names for things that are not commonly understood within the broader culture. As an example, consider a term such as "soul tie." It is a useful term to describe a very real situation, but it may sound alien to someone outside the church community. Take the time to explain or define any terms which may be new to your listeners.

f. We pretty much never use phrases like "Thus saith the Lord" or "God told me." Definitive language can be manipulative, and it excludes community discernment as well as the discernment of the person to whom you are ministering. Even if you are hearing very clearly from the Lord, God often reserves the interpretation and application of prophetic revelation for the body. When you share what you feel may be prophetic material, leave room for the discernment of those who are ultimately responsible for shepherding the body and for those who can test and help to interpret and apply what you are hearing or seeing. Share your prophetic impressions with phrases such as "I was feeling…," or "I was sensing that the Lord might be saying…does this resonate with you?". Submit the reception or rejection of the word to the discernment of those to whom the word applies and/or to responsible leadership.

It is exciting and also daunting to begin to minister in the power of the Holy Spirit. There is a serious learning curve when we move beyond being consumers of information to practitioners within our spheres of influence. May God bless you mightily with courage, hope, and great love, as you step out in faith!

APPENDIX E

Sample Prayers

THE FOLLOWING PRAYERS from the New Testament and other resources are helpful to healing ministry.

For wisdom: Ephesians 1:17–19a

"I keep asking that the God of our Lord Jesus Christ, the glorious Father, may give you the Spirit of wisdom and revelation, so that you may know him better. I pray that the eyes of your heart may be enlightened in order that you may know the hope to which he has called you, the riches of his glorious inheritance in his holy people, and his incomparably great power for us who believe."

For strength: Ephesians 3:14–19

"For this reason I kneel before the Father, from whom every family in heaven and on earth derives its name. I pray that out of his glorious riches he may strengthen you with power through his Spirit in your inner being, so that Christ may dwell in your hearts through faith. And I pray that you, being rooted and established in love, may have power, together with all the Lord's holy people, to grasp how wide and long and high and deep is the love of Christ, and to know this love that surpasses knowledge—that you may be filled to the measure of all the fullness of God."

For knowledge and insight: Philippians 1:9–11

"And this is my prayer: that your love may abound more and more in knowledge and depth of insight, so that you may be able to discern what is best and may be pure and blameless for the day of Christ, filled with the fruit of righteousness that comes through Jesus Christ—to the glory and praise of God."

For love: 1 Thessalonians 3:11–13

"Now may our God and Father himself and our Lord Jesus clear the way for us to come to you. May the Lord make your love increase and overflow for each other and for everyone else, just as ours does for you. May he strengthen your hearts so that you will be blameless and holy in the presence of our God and Father when our Lord Jesus comes with all his holy ones."

For boldness: Acts 4:29–30

"Now, Lord, consider their threats and enable your servants to speak your word with great boldness. Stretch out your hand to heal and perform signs and wonders through the name of your holy servant Jesus."

A personal prayer for the beginning of a healing process or journey

"God, my systems are broken. My body, and mind, and will, and emotions hurt in ways I cannot fix. Sometimes I care, and sometimes I don't. Sometimes I want to be fixed, and sometimes I just think that the process would be too hard, or hurt to badly, or be too disruptive, and might not make things better anyway. Sometimes I feel unworthy of being healed; like I deserve to suffer. Or maybe I think that at least suffering brings me some of the love and attention that I am so empty of, and so I don't even want to be healed. Or maybe it's been too long, and I've seen too much, and I am too tired or angry or sad to try any more. Jesus, I need more than what I have. Change me, so that I want to want your love more than what I have settled for. Give me the courage to see what is true, and to follow you wherever you lead me. Come, Holy Spirit, and bring the Kingdom of the Father."[42]

A prayer for protection, to be prayed before ministry

In the name of Jesus Christ of Nazareth, the Son of God who came in the flesh, and by the power of His cross and his blood, we bind up the power of any

---

[42] Amy Howard, *The Pain Eaters*, 2021.

evil spirits and command them to be silent, bound from interfering in any way in our ministry or prayers. We bind up the evil powers and spirits working or sent against us in the mighty name of Jesus Christ of Nazareth. We break any curses, hexes or spells sent against us and declare them null and void. We break the assignments of any spirits sent against us and send them to Jesus to deal with them as He will. Lord, we ask You to bless our enemies by sending Your Holy Spirit to lead them to repentance and conversion. We ask for the protection of the shed blood of Jesus Christ over _____.

Thank You, Lord, for Your protection and for sending Your warring angels to help us in the battle. We ask You to guide us in our prayers and to share with us Your Spirit's power and compassion. Amen.[43]

A prayer following ministry, for cleansing and renewal

Lord Jesus, thank You for sharing with us Your wonderful ministry of healing and deliverance. Thank You for Your healing—the healings we have witnessed today, and all healing that we cannot yet see. We realize that the sickness and evil we encounter is more than our humanity can bear, so cleanse us of any sadness, negativity, or despair that we may have picked up. If our ministry has tempted us to anger, impatience or lust, cleanse us of those temptations and replace them with love, joy, and peace. If any evil spirits have attached themselves to us or oppressed us in any way, we command them to depart—now—and go straight to Jesus Christ for Him to deal with you as He will.

Come Holy Spirit: renew us—fill us anew with Your power, Your life and Your joy. Strengthen us where we have felt weak and clothe us with Your light. Fill us with life. Lord Jesus, please send your Your holy angels to minister to us and our families—guard us and protect us from all sickness, harm, and accidents. (Give us a safe trip home.) We praise you You now and forever, Father, Son and Holy Spirit, and we ask these things in Jesus' Holy Name that he He may be glorified. Amen.[44]

---

[43] Inspired by the prayer of protection from Christian Healing Ministry, available at Christianhealingmin.org

[44] Modified from a prayer from Christian Healing Ministry, available at Christianhealingmin.org

Appendix E: Sample Prayers

A prayer to be set free from co-dependency

"Lord, I want my joy, my deep sense of well-being, to be free. It is wound around [name(s)]. I cannot fix them, or save them, or prevent their pain. I choose right now to give You each of these people, their pain, their happiness, their entire lives, and I cut free from them in the mighty name of Jesus Christ. I hand to You, at the cross, my guilt for failing them, my judgments of myself and others, my anger and resentment, and theirs. (Feel free to add any other sin, pain, or injuries to your prayer here, and release each of them, by name, to the One who loves you best.) Come, friend, and heal my soul where it has been wounded by carrying things and people that were too heavy for me. Thank You for freedom. I love You."[45]

For health of body and soul

"May God the Father bless you, God the Son heal you, God the Holy Spirit give you strength. May God the holy and undivided Trinity guard your body, save your soul, and bring you safely to his heavenly country; where he lives and reigns for ever and ever. Amen."[46]

---

[45] Amy Howard, *The Pain Eaters*, 2021.

[46] From *The Book of Common Prayer* (Anglican Liturgy Press, 2019), 233.

Bibliography & Sources for Further Study

The Anglican Church of North America. *To Be a Christian: An Anglican Catechism.* Wheaton, IL: Crossway, 2020.

Bergner, Mario. *Setting Love in Order.* Grand Rapids, MI: Hamewith Books, 1995.

Bickle, Mike. *Growing in the Prophetic.* Lake Mary, FL: Charisma House, 1996, 2008.

The Book of Common Prayer. Anglican Liturgy Press, 2019.

Fiske, Charles. *Back to Christ.* London: Longmans, Green and Co., 1917.

Frost, Jack. *Experiencing Father's Embrace.* Shippensburg, PA: Destiny Image, 2002.

Also available: teaching DVDs and Manual (MP4 download) from Shiloh Place Ministries, www.shilohplace.org.

Kolber, Aundi. *Try Softer: A Fresh Approach to Move Us out of Anxiety, Stress, and Survival Mode--and into a Life of Connection and Joy.* Carol Stream: IL, Tyndale Refresh, 2020.

Kreider, Alan. *The Patient Ferment of the Early Church: The Improbable Rise of Christianity in the Roman Empire.* Grand Rapids, MI: Baker Academic, 2016.

Ladd, George. *A Theology of the New Testament.* Grand Rapids, MI: Eerdmans, 1974.

Leech, Kenneth. *Soul Friend.* Harrisburg, PA: Morehouse Publishing, 1977.

Lozano, Neal. *Unbound.* Grand Rapids, MI: Baker Book House Co., 2003.

MacNutt, Francis. *Healing.* Notre Dame, IN: Ave Maria Press, 1974, 2006.

See also: Christian Healing Ministries, www.christianhealingmin.org (This is the webpage of Judith and the late Francis MacNutt.)

Payne, Leanne. *The Healing Presence.* Grand Rapids, MI: Hamewith Books, 1995.

Ramsey, Michael. *The Gospel and the Catholic Church.* Peabody, MA: Hendrickson Publishers Marketing, LLC, 2009.

Schmemann, Alexander. *For the Life of the World.* St. Vladimir's Seminary Press, 1997.

Thompson, Curt. *The Deepest Place: Suffering and the Formation of Hope.* Grand Rapids, MI: Zondervan, 2023.

Van der Kolk, Bessel. *The Body Keeps the Score: Brain, Mind and Body in the Healing of Trauma.* New York, NY: Penguin Random House, 2015.

Wimber, John. *Power Healing.* San Francisco: Harper and Row, 1987.

About the Author

Amy Howard is the director of Encounter Culture Missions Collaborative, a teaching, equipping, and micro-church movement formed to provide catalytic life-transforming weekends, follow-up training to replicate discipling cultures of transformation, and then coaching for leaders and ordinary believers in disciple-making. Amy is also an author and regular conference speaker, and she, her husband, and their six boys currently reside on their homestead in New Hampshire.

Made in the USA
Middletown, DE
01 December 2024

65536665R00064